Rare Encounters
with Ordinary Birds

Rare Encounters
with Ordinary Birds

Notes from a Northwest Year

Lyanda Lynn Haupt

SASQUATCH BOOKS
SEATTLE

Printed in Canada
Distributed in Canada by Raincoast Books, Ltd.
07 06 05 04 03 02 01   5 4 3 2 1

Cover illustration: Stan Fellows
Cover and interior design: Karen Schober
Interior illustrations: Linda Feltner
Interior design: Karen Schober
Copy editor: Erin Moore

Library of Congress Cataloging in Publication Data

Haupt, Lyanda Lynn.
   Rare encounters with ordinary birds : notes from a Northwest year /
Lyanda Lynn Haupt.
      p.cm.
   ISBN 1-57061-302-8
      1. Bird watching--Northwest, Pacific. 2. Birds--Northwest, Pacific.
I. Title.

QL683.N75 H38 2001
598'.07'234795--dc21

Sasquatch Books
615 Second Avenue
Seattle, Washington 98104
(206) 467-4300
www.SasquatchBooks.com
books@SasquatchBooks.com

For my parents, Jerry and Irene
—with love and gratitude

Contents

INTRODUCTION *9*

1   FIRST BIRD *13*

2   AN INVASION OF OWLS *23*

3   THE PRESENCE OF BIRDS: A VERY NEW LIFE LIST *33*

4   THE THRUSH AND THE FAERIE *47*

5   CORMORANT PROBLEM *59*

6   THE BIRDWATCHER'S BOOK OF SECRETS *79*

7   WHEN GOOD WOODPECKERS GO BAD *85*

8   THE PACIFIC-SLOPE FLYCATCHER: A NEW SPECIES, SORT OF *93*

9   THE HIDDEN BLUE GROUSE *103*

10   THE SECRET LIVES OF VAUX'S SWIFT *111*

11   WINTER WREN: THOUGHTS ON VOICE AND PLACE *125*

12   SPARROWS AS MOTHERS *135*

13   ONE-EYED DUNLIN *143*

14   YOUNG LOVE: A BACK-TO-SCHOOL STORY *149*

15   POSTCARDS FROM THE MAYAN RUINS 157

16   CROW STORIES *167*

17   BIRD VISION *181*

Evening Grosbeak

Introduction

One day when I was in fourth grade my class took a field trip to the University of Washington's arboretum. In a tree next to our walking trail, I saw a small gathering of autumn birds.

"Look," I whispered to Mrs. Rae, our teacher, "Evening Grosbeaks." She gave me a strange look. "See?" I pointed. "Evening Grosbeaks."

Our family saw grosbeaks in our backyard at home all the time. A field guide to birds sat on the table by sliding glass doors that led to a small patio surrounded by trees: mountain ash, maples, and Douglas firs. My younger sister and I would find the paintings in the book that matched the grosbeaks and other birds that frequented this miniature forest, try to tell the males from the females.

Mrs. Rae queried our trip leader, one of the arboretum's volunteer docents. "What are those birds?"

"Oh, those are Evening Grosbeaks," the guide instructed, and over the rest of the students' giggles (*gross*-beak—we were fourth-graders, after all), she gave a little lesson, explaining how the birds use their thick bills to eat seeds.

"How did you know that?" Mrs. Rae squinted at me when we resumed walking, and I hardly knew what to say. How did she *not* know? I have always remembered that day, the day I discovered that it is not necessarily "normal" to know a bird's name.

At home that evening I watched the grosbeaks from a quiet haunt in the grass. With binoculars I could see the gold on the male bird's flanks, which even in the shadowy dusk held a glow, and looked terribly soft. Naturally, I did not know then that twenty years later an Evening Grosbeak I was banding would bite my right index finger down to the bone, requiring a tetanus shot from a grumpy nurse. But back in the fourth grade I had a strange sense, though I could not have expressed it at the time, that this bird was *mine.* The grosbeak and I had a solitary understanding, a relationship that when I'd left for school that morning had been ordinary, but now, I knew, was set apart. I watched and watched.

Birds will give you a window, if you allow them. They will show you secrets from another world, fresh vision that, though avian, can accompany you home and alter your life. They will do this for you, even if you don't know them by name—though such knowing is a thoughtful gesture. They will do this for you if you watch them.

European Starling

First Bird

There is a game birders play on New Year's Day called "Bird of the Year." The very first bird you see on the first day of the new year is your theme bird for the next 365 days. It might seem a curious custom, but people who watch birds regularly are always contriving ways to keep themselves interested. This is one of those ways. You are given the possibility of creating something extraordinary—

a Year of the Osprey, Year of the Pileated Woodpecker, Year of the Trumpeter Swan. This game is an inspiration to place yourself in natural circumstances that will yield a heavenly bird, blessing your year, your perspective, your imagination, your spirit. *New year, first bird.*

This year my fresh little baby, just four weeks old, is tucked softly between my husband and me in bed early New Year's morning. I can hear them breathing—Tom, Claire, Ani the cat, Isabel the Australian Shepherd—all asleep. As my baby's only food source, I am stuck to this snug winter cottage where she lies wrapped and dreaming in flannel. There will be, this New Year's Day, no sneaking off to some fabulously promising birdish locale.

I consider our cozy home in a suburb of Seattle. In spite of our proximity to the city, we see incredible birds here—Bald Eagles, Great Blue Herons, a Cooper's Hawk one day, a Band-Tailed Pigeon. Even the common birds we see every day have some fine avian qualities—the intelligence of the Steller's Jays, the seeming cheerful industriousness of the Black-capped Chickadee, the limitless sociability of the Bushtit. None of these would be too shabby as a theme bird for my first year of motherhood. I pull on Tom's robe, sneak quietly out the side door, and look up expectantly.

In light of the dark shadow perched on our fence, I quickly decide to make up a few addenda to the "Bird of the Year" rules. The first bird you see *after 7 A.M.* is Bird of the Year. The first bird you see after your loved ones wake up. The first *native* bird . . . I am usually quite good at lying to myself, but even for me this would be just too blatant. Here before me sits a bird that ecologists refer to as "sky-rat." Year of the European Starling it is.

The starling was introduced to North America in the late nineteenth century by an "acclimatization society" hoping to populate the new world with every bird mentioned in the Shakespearean canon. This is one of those Bird Myths that is actually true. The society's leader, Eugene Schieffelin, possessed two passions—ornithology and Shakespeare. He combed the plays and sonnets, turning up a single, unmemorable line in part I of *Henry IV:* "I'll have a starling shall be taught to speak nothing but 'Mortimer.'" This obscure and hapless mention was enough to fuel Schieffelin's resolve.

First attempts to transport the starling failed, but in 1890 one hundred birds survived travel by sea from Europe, were released in New York's Central Park, and established a small population. By 1940 there were few places left in North America where the starling had not been observed. The Northwest was one of them.

It's fascinating to read the early literature on the birdlife of this region. In Ralph Hoffman's 1927 account covering all Pacific Northwest birds, starlings are not even mentioned. It's an idyll in time that seems so far and impossible now, yet it has been only a matter of decades. Reports of winter starlings began to appear in Seattle in 1949, and the first locally observed rearing of young was recorded in 1962, two years before I was born. Now there are tens of thousands of starlings here. Autumn flocks blacken the evening skies, and even starling haters find their cloudlike movements astonishing, if not beautiful, as they swarm precisely in dusky arcs.

The native breeding range of the European Starling covers Europe, a good portion of Eurasia, the British Isles and Scandinavia, and the Middle East. Their winter range stretches to north Africa. Besides North America, regions colonized in recent times by population expansion include South Africa, Australia, New Zealand and its surrounding islands, Jamaica, and parts of the West Indies. Even so, it is estimated that roughly one-third of the world population of European Starlings resides here, in North America. Two hundred million individual birds have sprung from the handful that were released in Central Park just a century ago.

There is no doubt that the habitat changes wrought by European settlement, and continuing today with relentless suburban sprawl, have contributed to the starling's success in this country. While it may have been a fruitful colonizer in any case, it is doubtful that the increase in starling numbers and range would have been so vast without rapid landscape changes creating the sorts of expanses on which it thrives. Starlings love mown grass and grazed fields, the warm and sheltered roosts that human habitations offer. They avoid only a few types of landscape—mostly deep forests and deserts, the kinds of places that humans tend not to live.

For the most part, the starling is an ecological disaster, competing aggressively and successfully with native birds for food and, more importantly, nest sites. It is believed that starlings have a detrimental effect on several of these species, particularly cavity-nesting birds such as wood-peckers and bluebirds. They readily exploit disturbed habitats and varied food sources, advantages that over-whelm the few controls on their population—predation, disease, bad weather. Some birds and mammals includ-ing accipiters, falcons, owls, weasels, rats, dogs, and cats, do manage to eat a few starlings. But none consider the starling a major food source, and it is doubtful that pre-dation makes much of an impact on starling numbers.

The ecological effects of the starling, though, are not quite so starkly cut. Starlings are known to eat cutworms, a horticultural menace. Some prominent ornithologists believe that the starling's impact on native birds is over-stated. Rachel Carson penned an early essay in 1939 enti-tled "How About Citizenship Papers for the Starling?" in which she suggested that starlings have such a positive agricultural impact that we should stop viewing them with suspicion and grant them official residency. (Of course, this was sixty years ago, and there were not nearly so many starlings then.) Because they are a non-native, invasive species, starlings are afforded no legal protection, mak-ing them accessible, abundant, and hassle-free research subjects. As such, starlings have contributed significantly to our understanding of avian migration strategies, flight mechanics, endocrine systems, and other aspects of basic bird biology. Starlings are also wildly intelligent and, at second glance, quite beautiful.

The species' scientific name is *Sturnus vulgaris*. *Vulgaris* translates poorly. Some anti-starlingists feel the implications of the name suit the bird perfectly, but the Latin simply means common, not actually vulgar. *Sturnus* means starling, possibly from the Latin *sterne*, star. The name might refer to the four-pointed silhouette of the starling in flight—bill, triangular wing tip, tail squared to a point, second wing. Star-ling, "little star."

When starlings leave the nest as fledglings, they have mousy brown bodies, somewhat pale throats and breasts, and dark bills. By late September all the birds are in their adult nonbreeding plumage. Green-black wings are outlined in buffy orange, the black bellies and shoulders spotted with pearl-white, the head streaked with these lighter colors. They look quite fresh and stunning.

Many bird species molt into a more colorful breeding plumage, but the starling's is acquired by wear. Pale feather colors are more susceptible to exposure, the effects of weather, light, and use. The white spots wear away and the orange wing outlines are trimmed, leaving an iridescent bird flecked with gold and jewel-toned in shimmering purple, green, and black. The bill turns bright yellow during the breeding season, and though the sexes look very much alike, you can amaze and impress your friends by telling them apart at close range with a secret birder's trick. The base of the female's bill is pink, the male's is blue—yes, pink for girls, blue for boys.

Starlings have unique, fun-to-watch foraging habits. While other birds look quite normal stepping about the yard, starlings walk with an exaggerated, vigorous gait, an actual waddle.

A particularly plastic species, starlings will eat nearly anything. Their largely invertebrate diet is supplemented by berries, nuts, seeds, cat food, and garbage. Raising three chickens in my own backyard, I have learned that corn scratch is regarded highly by starlings, when my rather uppity hens deign to allow the smaller birds into their yard.

In spite of the birds' eclectic diet, starling bodies seem particularly well adapted to invertebrate seeking. Compare them to robins, who also look for worms and insects in your backyard grasses. The starling bill is much pointier than a robin's, and very sharp. Rather than picking exposed prey, as robins do, starlings rigorously insert their bills into the ground, then use highly developed protractor muscles to open their mouths in the soil, creating a hole in which they can actually dig for little earth-dwellers. Watching small flocks for long periods, you can learn to pick out particular birds by their individual variations on this basic foraging style.

Some years ago, I worked on the East Coast as a raptor rehabilitator. Our center was established to treat and release injured birds of prey, but somehow birds of all feathers wound up at our doorstep, everything from a baby Ruby-throated Hummingbird to a Canada Goose with a bad limp. It was a house rule that we would not treat non-native "pest" species such as House Sparrows, pigeons, and, of course, starlings. Time and resources were just too scarce.

But what do you do when a knobby-kneed eight-year-old boy comes to you with an injured starling? His mother watches expectantly in the background as he strokes its back gently with one finger, looking extremely worried and sad, and asks you, near tears, "Can you take care of it?" Just what do you say? "Yeah, kid, I'll take care of that bird. Hand it over and I'll wring its scrawny neck." Here, a wider opportunity presents itself, one that transcends ecological or financial realities. Here is a child with an intact respect for life, and a rare opportunity to nurture that respect. Who among us does not still feel, in some small way, the mark made on our own quiet child heart by an injured bird that crossed our path?

A raptor center renegade, I set up a little hospital for these ecological misfits in the corner of my room at home, nursing them back to reasonable health, then returning them to their young benefactors with instructions for final fattening up and release.

It was under such circumstances that I came to raise my first baby starling. Biologist Bernd Heinrich writes, "If you seek contact with a wild bird that will bond, that will 'talk' (and even learn to sing tunes), and that will be practical to keep, I recommend adopting a starling. Mozart had one, and evidently he was extremely fond of it." I would have loved to discuss starling sentiments with Mozart, as I was utterly unprepared for the congenial, intelligent camaraderie offered by this little bird. Even after it was well fed, the juvenile starling, now completely feathered out, would run up and down the hall after me, wait impatiently outside the bathroom door for me, and read Proust over my shoulder. He would look me straight in the eye and "talk" for minutes at a time, imitating my intonation pattern.

Mimicry has an important place in starling biology. Birds in the starling family were described in detail by Aristotle in ancient Greece, where they were taught to imitate human voices. Individual starlings are able to amass repertoires of more than twenty bird songs, as well as inanimate sounds such as jackhammers and, more recently, cellular phones. Birds commonly mimicked include killdeer, robins, crows, gulls, and others, depending on the geographic wanderings of the particular starling. Instead of attempting to teach my small friend human words, I played tapes of my favorite bird songs over and over, Northwest voices that I missed during my tenure on the East Coast. Still a juvenile, the young starling learned to produce a convincing Wilson's Warbler and a passing Swainson's Thrush.

I do not harbor any falsely poetic feelings about the presence of starlings, or any blinders regarding their truly negative ecological impact. If I had a magic wand that would erase starlings from the face of North America, I would wave it now. But I certainly possess no such implement, and other less poetic means of starling eradication—poison, traps, birth control, removal of roost sites, blaring loudspeakers, and guns—continue to fail miserably.

E. O. Wilson wrote in *Biophilia*, his classic text on the innate human connection with the wider, living earth, "Every species is a magic well," a window onto all others. As an urban dweller I am forced to come to grips with the idea that I might turn to the starling as easily as any other species for lessons in living with and alongside birds and the natural world. I consider the unique landscape of the Pacific Northwest to be my wider home, but every day I live in an urban cottage, not an ancient forest, a coastal prairie, or a heavenly alpine meadow. Those places surround me, they are my authentic home, inhabited by the lives of astonishing birds. I like to think that in the widest sense we are in the presence of all these birds, always. But today, we start where we are.

I look back up at my Bird of the Year. Even in winter she is pretty, glinting with flecks of gold, iridescent black, purple, and green. Tom and Claire are up now, rustling about the coffeepot. I am hopeful, amazed already by the coming year. The starling will remind me, every day.

Snowy Owl

An Invasion of Owls

When I was seven years old, my mother cut a photograph from the local paper and read the caption with me. A Snowy Owl had appeared in a Seattle suburb near our home. It was pictured there, settled on someone's chimney. The large white bird filled the frame, round eyes looking directly into the camera. My mother's mind had lately settled lightly on birds. She'd purchased a field guide, and showed it happily to my sister and me, saying to us matter-of-factly that all homes should have one, and didn't we think so? She started to name and know the birds that populated our large backyard. Now this owl had appeared, resonating perfectly with her newfound interest.

My mom thought I should take the owl picture to school for show-and-tell, since the owl's appearance was quite unusual and its countenance vivid and appealing, even to first-graders, and even through the lens of the *Kent News Journal*'s weekend photographer. My offering got pasted onto our class bulletin board, earning me some kind of star. I visited the photo every school day, reaching up to pet the owl's two-dimensional head and looking into its eyes, which looked, always, straight back at me.

Twenty-five years later, Snowy Owls were showing up again in Seattle, just as they had appeared at somewhat regular intervals every six to eight years during the intervening quarter century. This time when they arrived, I worked at the Seattle Audubon office, where I received daily calls from excited and interested citizens reporting sightings or asking questions about the birds they'd seen. What joy to have work that considered talking on the phone about owls to be part of the job description.

The periodic invasion of the Northwest by Snowy Owls is based on complex ecological interactions between the owl and its lemming prey base on the arctic tundra, the Snowy's native home. In simplest terms, the arctic lemming population crashes episodically, resulting in an owl prey deficit. The paucity of lemmings drives many owls to lower latitudes, seeking basic sustenance.

Most of the Snowy Owls that settle for the winter in the Northwest will populate the tidal flats of coastal areas, and riverine deltas. Early bird chronicler William Leon Dawson, pondering the Pacific Northwest irruption in the winter of 1896-97, postulated that the Snowies "were especially noticeable upon the Tacoma tide-flats, since they reproduced on a miniature scale the tundra of their native haunts." And though the invading owls do seem to favor such places, numbers of them also find their way into the suburbs and the city, causing a great stir among passersby, most of whom have never seen an owl of any kind, let alone a striking and enormous, golden-eyed white owl that looks, from its perch atop a marble column adorning a turn-of-the-century bank building, like royalty.

The Snowy Owls that head south in search of food are the lowest on the owl totem pole—young birds, mostly males. The birds that we see during the invasion years all share characteristic immature plumage—striking white with vivid black barring. As adults Snowy Owls are nearly all white. While most avian species have bare parts (typically the feet and bill), Snowy Owls are entirely covered in feathers, from their nostrils to their toes, to fend off the arctic chill. The eyes are small, for an owl, but the color is unforgettable—a clear bright gold found nowhere else in nature.

Unfortunately, most of the much-heralded invading owls will not reach adulthood. Young birds, inexperienced hunters, unfamiliar territory. This is a recipe for starvation, and experts suggest that the majority of the birds will succumb over the course of an irruption winter, as these years of descending owls are termed in the ornithological literature. Owl corpses, however, are mysteriously difficult to come by, and in spite of the seeming ease achieved by winter-roosting Snowy Owls, the birds are by nature wary, and certainly claim some privacy when the time to die approaches. We don't really know what happens to them all.

Owls are not like other birds. I suppose one could say this about any avian tribe, but owls are particularly unlike, with layered dimensions of dissimilarity. Some of these reside in the physical objectivity of owl lives. Some we confer upon them in our human musings, preferences, and prejudices. Owls have a peculiar knowing way, a strict sense of personal space, a connoisseur's restful delight in their food, a certain repose, a remarkable capacity for necessary aggression. We don't need to anthropomorphize owls in order to feel some connection. But their silence, their nocturnal habits, their secret ways—all of this adds a layer of mystery on top of that which seems so familiar. Feathery soft eyelids on the same bird as the curved, impossibly sharp talons. We cannot take our eyes off an owl. They are all we can imagine them to be.

According to ornithologist Stanley Jewett in his 1953 *Birds of Washington*, the first incursion on record for the

Pacific Northwest is from the winter of 1889-90; the next is the one mentioned by Dawson, 1896-97, followed by 1908, and then in 1916, "the greatest flight of all." And how was such greatness measured? "The handsome plumage of the snowy owl," Jewett explains, "brings numerous specimens into the shops of taxidermists." Indeed, gun-toting birdwatchers of the early 1900s were only too happy to encounter a Snowy Owl. As Dawson puts it, "No opportunity is ever lost of killing one of these handsome midwinter visitors." In the great 1916 invasion, Fred Edwards of Tacoma had thirty owls brought to his shop for preparation; there were forty reported by a taxidermist in Bellingham, forty-one in Seattle, a hundred in Spokane.

"One might suppose," says Dawson, "from the number of specimens which adorn store windows and taxidermists' shops, that the bird is much more common than it really is." Normally one can expect that a bird killed in such numbers presupposes a level of commonality, and a healthy population that continues beyond the lifeless glass eyes of a specimen. In the case of a remarkable, conspicuous, and locally unusual bird such as the Snowy Owl, it is likely that nearly all of the birds that showed up in these turn-of-the-century invasions succumbed to hunters who sought a beautiful mounted trophy, or, just as likely, lumped any owl into the group of vermin that included wolves, coyotes, hawks, and eagles— all animals perceived to be at odds with human purposes, and therefore deserving of systematic destruction.

It wasn't until the 1920s that a more ecological perspective was introduced into conservation discourse, the bellwether for this shift being a hint at more tolerant attitudes toward the "vermin" predators. Even so, our relationship with owls continues to be fraught with a complexity and prejudice that we have not overcome. Written in the 1950s, Stanley Jewett's owl commentaries contain passages in which the worth of a species is measured entirely against human preferences. Thus, the food habits of the loquacious Screech Owl "recommend it to the protection of man," the order of preference being "insects, mice, and birds." "Good" owls eat insects and rodents; "bad" owls eat birds that we consider pretty, game birds that we prefer to kill ourselves, or domestic poultry. Today, many farmers in the West continue to shoot and poison avian predators as a matter of course. And here in the Pacific Northwest, the Northern Spotted Owl, an unwitting symbol of ancient forest conservation, continues to be a political pariah. Their soft, small bodies are still found shot and hung, lynching-style, in the national forests by self-proclaimed "anti-environmentalists," many of whom have poor owl identification skills and kill any owl in their paths, including the politically innocent Barred and Great Horned Owls.

For the general public of the Pacific Northwest, the Snowy Owl irruptions may be the single most visible and edifying bird event. The media attention that follows the

Snowy Owl invasions is, in Bird News, singular in its enthusiasm. The only other birds to achieve anywhere near the Snowies' celebrity are Stewart and Belle, the Peregrine Falcons with a permanent video camera fixed on their nest atop the Washington Mutual Tower in downtown Seattle.

Most of the owl media coverage is lighthearted and visual—"weather art," my onetime-photojournalist husband calls it. Some of the newspapers offer a series of articles that increase in depth for a week or two, before dropping the topic of owls completely. (The owls will, after all, be around most of the winter. The newspapers don't give our attention spans quite that much credit.) Articles might cover the lemming theory, the predicted demise of the owls, quote some wildlife experts and Audubon office workers, and attempt some kind of statement on the human place in such ecological happenings. Meanwhile, amateur ornithologists set off to the far ends, keeping track of the owls, keeping watch, and setting the image in their minds to hold them through the owl-less years.

The tallies of birds in the Snowy Owl invasion years these days are kept in field notebooks that record numbers of live owls witnessed, rather than in a taxidermist's ledger recording numbers of corpses deposited for preparation. In spite of the drastic ecological lapses that characterize our species, we have moved, in a relatively short time, from accepting the shooting of a Snowy Owl as a matter of course—because it is beautiful, because it is an owl, or because it is *there*—to finding such an action unthinkable.

Here is evidence. During the recent Snowy Owl invasion, one of the birds roosts for days in a tall Douglas fir at the edge of a local elementary school's play yard. I bring a telescope for students to observe the bird, while we talk a little about owls in general and this owl in particular. The third-grade students at this inner-city school with a reputation for rowdiness are hushed and rapt. "I love the Snowy Owl," one boy tells me soberly. Another young student has a particularly intent gaze. "I'm talking to the owl with my mind," she says.

On the following Thursday an Audubon constituent calls the office reporting a Snowy near her home on a bluff overlooking Lake Washington. A couple of office mates, volunteers, and I pack into my little car, and we all go to have a look. A man engaged in home truck repair sees us pull the spotting scope out of the trunk and begin to scan the trees. "Lookin' for the white owl? Up there," he points strongly to the middle of a tall corner fir, until we all say that we see. "Been there for hours." He and some other neighbors wander over. Our scope is suddenly very popular, and for once, we birdwatchers seem useful rather than merely eccentric.

Here is evidence. This greasy-handed man with an NRA sticker on his pickup window peers through my scope. "A snow owl? God. Gorgeous." He goes back to his repair job, but in ten minutes comes back and asks sheepishly,

"Can I look again?" *Hi, pretty snow owl*, he whispers, bent over the scope. My birdwatcher friends and I exchange secret smiles.

The Presence of Birds:
A Very New Life List

Squinting across the waves, I make quick pencil notes in my little book. Brown Pelican. Surf Scoter. Double-crested Cormorant. "What are you doing?" Tom asks.

"Nothing." *Common Loon.*

"No. You're doing something. I see you. You're writing, and you're being sneaky."

"Honey, I am not being sneaky. I'm making a life list here." *Bald Eagle!*

"But you've already seen all these birds. *I've* seen all these birds and I'm not even a birder."

It's a gorgeous day on the Washington coast. Though it's late August, we feel the sharp breeze that is nearly ever-present on this rocky beach, and the ocean is gray, sparkling darkly. I am afraid to tell Tom the truth.

"Well, it's not my list."

He waits.

"It's hers." I point to my enormous belly. I figure if I'm matter-of-fact I can slip this by him.

"Hers?"

"Our baby's."

Tom looks at me straight and long. He stares at the water, and back at me. Finally, he speaks in a gentle voice, as if he believes me to be unstable, and any harsh words will send me completely over the edge.

"Honey." He touches me sweetly on the shoulder, breaking the news. "Honey, our baby isn't born yet. She can't have a life list."

Undaunted by Tom's bad attitude, I carry on with the task at hand. "Look, sweetie! An Osprey! Sanderlings! Black Oystercatchers! Oh, what a good day for our little girl."

A "life list" is a record of all the bird species one has ever seen. Birders might keep various lists—a backyard list, a state list, a year list, an international list—but the *real* list, the one that serious birders from this neck of the world refer to when they speak of their own life lists, includes birds seen within the parameters of the

American Birding Association's official North American list area, which includes Canada and the forty-nine continental United States, the French Islands of St. Pierre et Miquelon, and their adjacent waters. Six hundred species puts you squarely in the ranks of the hard-core.

It might seem innocuous enough, but this list keeping can easily get out of hand. I heard a story about a couple whose birding vacation in Arizona ended in divorce after he spotted a bird she needed for her own life list and, in the spirit of bitter competition, refused to point her in the bird's direction. I know of birders who, in addition to placing a check mark next to a new bird on their list (a so-called "lifer"), will also enter a dollar amount. This represents the expenses involved in chasing down the rare bird—airfare, motor inn, rental car, fast food. In a term borrowed from British birders, such people are referred to as "twitchers," an allusion to the check marks or "twitches" compulsively added as rarities are chased across the nation.

More ecologically oriented birders must officially go on record as being opposed to mere twitching, where birders swoop down in their rented car, take a quick glance at the bird they seek, gasp and proclaim it beautiful (or not), twitch, and swoop away again. Such a practice, it is argued, reduces birds to the two-dimensionality of baseball cards, and utterly neglects matters of true import—behavior, ecology, conservation status, the honing of honest observational skills, respect, love. Still, many holistic naturalists have some of the longest life lists I know.

As much as I try to stay away from the list-or-not-to-list fray, it is impossible to avoid the bird-listing question entirely. Rank strangers who spy you with a pair of binoculars about your neck want to know if you keep one; friend birders are curious about how many species you have seen, eager to compare notes. Responding to such inquiries, I always lie. "I don't keep a list," I say. It seems that the idea of a list says something about a person, and about the way that person interacts with birds—something not necessarily true.

In terms of definitions, maintenance of a life list appears to be the deed that catapults a person from being a "birdwatcher"—someone who enjoys birds and even knows the names of species that frequent their yard or summer cottage—to someone who actively, and perhaps competitively, seeks birds, for fun, challenge, sport, or love. Some suggest a loose continuum from birdwatcher to birder to ornithologist. I have to think this idea of a linear progression is mostly misguided.

Some backyard birders know a great deal more about the natural history of avian species than do serious "birders." Some ornithologists can identify very few birds beyond the couple of species that they might study in depth for their academic research. Some birders are holistic in their approach, engaged in the many intellectual dimensions of the ornithological and ecological sciences, as well as being brilliant at avian identification. Some birders are not. Some appropriate birds according to their knowledge of taxonomic order, some by a looser aesthetic sense based on size and shape, some entirely by song and vocalizations.

In this latter group, I know a birdsong expert who categorizes vocalizations into common-sense types of sound, such as buzzing, warbling, and trills. Another, a concert pianist, classifies the birdsong that reaches his trained ears according to a musical scheme, with attention to pitch and timbre, complex phrasing, and rhythmic variation.

I know people who can, at a glance, identify nearly any North American bird that enters their peripheral vision, but once they name it can tell you nothing further about it. Others can name very few, but hold an intimate knowledge of the lives of certain species based on observation, deep and careful attendance over time. We twitter over labels for all these manners of watching, and we fail. Human interaction with birds is a highly individual art.

I have come to believe that although anyone might learn to identify birds with moderate proficiency, some people have a predisposition toward it, a disposition that others lack utterly. My father-in-law, Al, is an academic by nature and trade, with a remarkable mind. He is able to catalogue minute details in his own fields of history and literature, details that he calls to mind with stunning accuracy. My in-laws moved to the Northwest a couple of years ago, into a house by a stream with maples and willows and lots of birds. Since they expressed interest, I bought them a field guide.

At first when Al called me with questions about the birds he was seeing, I fully expected long and intricate accounts of the species in question. Instead, he would say something like "What is the bird we saw in our tree today? It was medium-sized and brown."

"Did it have any markings? Anything on the head or wings?"

"I don't think so, but I can't say for sure."

"Did it hang upside-down?" I'd ask. "Was it part of a flock of birds that looked the same?" He wasn't sure.

We share varieties of this conversation over and over again. I find it both endearing and terribly curious. Here is a man who can recite minutiae from some obscure book on early American history he read twelve years ago, but can't describe with any sort of reliable accuracy the bird that perched in front of his nose that afternoon. I have to remind myself that this is, of course, a very normal condition. The idea that one must note specific subtle marks and behaviors in order to identify a bird is something that, for most people, is *learned* with varying degrees of effort.

My mother is another case altogether. Not the least bit bookish, she will tell me that she saw a bird alone by the water with a white breast and brown back that bobbed up and down while leaning forward. *Spotted Sandpiper*. A small hawk with a square head and long tail in the tree; it stood up straight on long, skinny yellow legs. *Sharp-shinned Hawk*. She has a gift for seeing the salient points that might differentiate one bird from another, even if she doesn't know what bird it is. And she somehow knows that a bird's color, what most of us would think to start with, is not necessarily the most helpful thing.

I think of this as a kind of Bird Aptitude, and people who have it are able to learn birds quickly and easily. It's not unlike a math aptitude. I remember a young man, Clinton, who sat in the back of my high school trigonometry class, rolling those strange many-sided dice used by Dungeons and Dragons aficionados. He scarcely paid attention to the instructor, but could quickly whip out assignments and pass tests with accuracy and a certain finesse. Meanwhile, I worked and worked, racking my mathematically simple mind. We both did tolerably well in the class, but for Clinton it was effortless, while for me it was terrible trouble, and I utterly lacked *finesse*.

The very nice thing about all this, of course, is that the variety of birdwatching personalities, while not all necessarily suited to a life of radical bird-listing, are perfectly suited, in one way or another, to the habit of watching birds. I have heard that learning a bird's name is a starting point to further knowledge, but I think this point comes earlier still, in the first observation of an individual bird. In the field one day I saw two young women with *Peterson's Field Guide to Western Birds*. I lifted my binoculars to the nice duck-filled pond before us, and innocuously eavesdropped. They were studying their book with rich attention, comparing various plates to the bird before them, a rather common small duck called a Green-winged Teal. The duck sat obligingly on the pond as they cross-checked its various marks, comparing it with the plates in their book. They were quietly jubilant, patting each other's arms and smiling, as they correctly concluded the teal's identity.

There is a point in identifying a new species at which you understand suddenly, almost viscerally—yes, that is *what it is*. I felt a pang of jealousy at the newness of their discovery, remembering the first bird beyond the confines of my backyard that I tediously identified on my own, the Pelagic Cormorant. There is a quiet exhilaration that comes in discovering for yourself—using binoculars, field guide, your innate wits, and a willing subject—the name of a bird new to you. There is a change, a shift, and it feels somehow mutual, something between you and the bird. With practice, the process of identification becomes less tedious, and eventually second nature.

Second nature, of course, unless you are someone who cannot identify birds, not at all, not ever. These people exist. In a coastal bird class I taught recently, a group of about twenty of us were watching shorebirds on the Oregon coast. I will admit that shorebirds are a particularly challenging group, lots of small birds in shades of brown scampering about on the rocks and sand. Their identification often lies in the intricate details of particular feathers. But this was a beginning class, and we were just picking out some of the easiest birds. On the beach was a tall bird with a straight longish bill called a Greater Yellowlegs, easy to remember since its long legs are truly lemon-yellow. A Whimbrel, another large bird with a long curved bill and non-yellow legs, was also present. There were several small Semi-palmated Plovers, perhaps the cutest of North American shorebirds: black-backed and white-bellied, with a broad brown band across the breast, orange bill, and enormous eyes. Amid all these wandered a mixed group of Western and Least Sandpipers that, because they are difficult to tell apart at first, we didn't worry about too much.

We had been with the birds for nearly an hour, and had the chance for careful observation. Most of the people in the group got a handle on these birds quite quickly, and started to take good field notes on their physical and behavioral differences. But there was one woman in the group who could not tell the birds apart at all: not the big from the small, not the distinctly dark brown plovers from the mottled sandpipers; she could not even get a sense that the yellowlegs, easily a foot taller than the Least Sandpipers, was actually a different species. I was baffled. One bird was huge, another was tiny. Could she see that? "I know that you think you can tell these birds apart," she told me earnestly, "but they all look like small brown birds to me." The rest of the class and I all tried not to stare in disbelief. She thought all of us were nuts.

But the great thing about birdwatching is this—we all loved it, we all had a great day. While part of the class worked on their notes and some of the more serious students started to focus on distinguishing between the Westerns and Leasts, the Hopeless Identifier Woman pulled her broad-brimmed straw hat further down over her forehead. She took out her notebook, fit a Mona Lisa–like smile upon her lips, and composed fourteen lines in iambic pentameter, an actual shorebird sonnet. Later, she read it to the class as we recouped in a shady park, and we all clapped.

I like to think that Claire and I do not "chase" birds. Nor do we "twitch." Even so, now that Claire is four months old, her life list is quite substantial. In our backyard she enjoys the presence of Northern Flickers, Steller's Jays, American Robins, and Dark-eyed Juncos. At the Puget Sound beaches near our home she observes Horned Grebes, Red-breasted Mergansers, Common and Barrow's Goldeneyes, and her personal favorite—small flocks of the very delicate Brant goose. At Green Lake Park she adds a variety of waterfowl—Gadwall, American Wigeon, Pied-billed Grebe, American Coot, and even a lone Eurasian Wigeon. She has seen, in her special baby way, six species of gull.

Now that my little project is out in the open, I flaunt it to irk Tom for fun.

"Excellent," I announce on a recent ferry trip. "Claire doesn't have Red-necked Grebe yet."

"She doesn't *have* anything," Tom informs me, getting a bit self-righteous. He starts making rules. "She can't have a list until she can identify the birds herself."

Well, that seems a bit strict to me. Besides, I firmly believe that Claire can see and assimilate the world's creatures, even if she can't yet speak their names. I hold her up to the ferry railing, blinking in the wind. Next to us a man is pointing at a dark flock of birds floating on the water. "See the duckies?" he coos to his toddler. Unwilling to chance Claire's becoming tainted by such ambiguity, I whisper, "Look, sweetie, White-winged Scoters." Claire giggles and opens her mouth wide in a goofy, toothless grin that melts my heart.

Why am I keeping a life list of birds for my small daughter? I make up all kinds of reasons for Tom, just to see what he'll say: *I want Claire to get ahead of all the hotshot birder tots she'll meet in preschool. My birder ex-boyfriend's child is three years old and has an unfair advantage on Claire—she must catch up! I want to prepare her for a brilliant ornithological career. I want her to stabilize her ego via an impressive life list.*

None of these are true.

The real reason is simple. In my experience, birds are as fine and appropriate a lens through which to assimilate life as anything else. A list of the birds one has seen can unspool a ribbon of detail, the chance occurrences that create our singular lives, the minutiae that might be lost in the clutter were it not for this unique kind of record. Claire is only four months old, but looking at her life list of birds, the discerning reader might apprehend a great deal about the world that has shaped her development as a young human. Claire was born and has lived in the Pacific Northwest *(Varied Thrush, Oregon Junco)*. She dwells near water *(Brant, Horned Grebe)* and has ventured out upon its openness *(Marbled Murrelet)*. She has visited the wet forests that characterize her home *(Winter Wren)*. Claire has a large tree outside her nursery window, connecting her small yard with nearby conifers and apple trees *(Steller's Jay, Northern Flicker)*. Claire's wider home has maintained enough ecological integrity to support the largest of avian predators *(Bald Eagle)* and there are fish *(Osprey)*. Claire has gazed at watery coastlines and has lifted her small eyes skyward at the flash of a large, dark shadow *(Great Blue Heron)*. The absence of certain birds is just as telling. Though she may sense the inkling of warmth, the lengthening of days that has us all dreaming desperately of spring, Claire has, so far, been a winter child, knowing this season only *(there is no Rufous Hummingbird yet, no Yellow Warbler. . .)*.

What this list says is that my new daughter has lived, already, in the unique company of wild, nonhuman beings. That her life is entwined, inextricably, with a wider natural world, a world that will continue to reveal itself, effortlessly, over time.

I remember, when I was in college, overhearing my mother saying to her friends, "Yes, Lyanda, she is quite a birdwatcher. "Mother," I was indignant, "It's *birder*, not birdwatcher." Will Claire be a birder? If it brings her joy

I certainly hope she is, but in truth I care not a whit. My wish for my new daughter is that she will be a true *watcher* of birds. Or perhaps a watcher of mushrooms, or beetles, or snakes, or rocks. That she will choose her own lens into the natural world, know it deeply and well, with a wisdom cultivated in travel, in experience of home, with friends, with love, through the whole of her life.

But for now, I keep this list. I love to think of the birds—including the common birds, the feathered arbiters of everyday life—that await Claire as this life list grows. I see, in my mind, the species that will grace and unfold her days, as she lives in the presence of birds.

The Thrush and the Faerie

I have been told, though I do not remember it myself,
that I saw, whether once or many times I do not know,
a supernatural bird in the corner of the room.

—WILLIAM BUTLER YEATS

When I visit my parents' house I do not have to worry about what to have for dinner, or when to do the laundry, or what time to get up in the morning, or how I will manage to make the coffee before absolutely keeling over from needing a cup because, of course, the coffee will be ready when I rise. My parents' smoothly running household has the added bonus of sitting directly in the middle of ten wooded acres. Wet, dripping, western Washington forest, quite respectable second-growth woodlands, Douglas fir and Western hemlock, tangles of ferns and mosses and birds.

Their land abuts the local watershed, a lush 600 acres that, for the most part, humans are not allowed to roam. The watershed is wide enough for the small herd of elk that live there and sometimes venture into the yard and lettuce frame; for the coyotes that we can hear howling so beautifully, one of which ate Jezabel, my mother's purebred Somali cat. It is deep enough for owls, not just the Great Horned Owls we hear quite regularly, but also a Northern Pygmy-Owl, and once I am sure I heard a Long-eared.

The Northwest forest birds abound here in such glory that a walk ten feet from the back door makes me realize with a start the impoverished birdlife of my own daily suburban existence. Here are Pileated Woodpeckers, Red-breasted Sapsuckers, Purple Finches, Black-throated Gray Warblers buzzing and nesting in the summer, and, it seems, all the Rufous Hummingbirds in the world. Below them on the ground, walking warily and brightly in pumpkin and navy feathers, are the Varied Thrushes. Picking through the leaves, skirting the edges, then flying straight back into the forest.

I am staying a few nights, a sweet visit and personal vacation. Just after sunrise this morning, I opened the window wide and went back to bed. Even with the window closed, I could hear the Varied Thrushes. Now it was as if they were perched in every corner of the room, creating those strange harmonic chords that float, and live, and seem almost, but never quite, to end. I listened forever, half-asleep.

There is a legend that warns wanderers of Northwest forests to keep their heads when hearing the preternatural song of the Varied Thrush. If you are alone, if there is a veil of fog hanging from the coniferous branches at a certain slant, the song lulls you into a frame of mind that makes you susceptible to abduction by faeries. Evidently, they will caper you away to their own faery-world, where years may pass in the space of a normal hour.

If you have never heard this song in the dripping depths of a coastal forest, then you may be forgiven your incredulity, or outright dismissal of this well-founded legend. But if you have heard such a song in such a place, if you have given yourself over to listening just a fraction longer than we ever seem to listen to anything in our busy millennial hours, then I dare you to dismiss the possibility outright.

When I was in my twenties, I would boldly backpack alone into the ancient forests of the Olympic Peninsula, vexing my mother and anyone else who could think to worry. I would listen to the Varied Thrush song rising through the woods at twilight, gently resisting the spell. The faeries might keep a person, particularly a fresh young woman, for long periods of time, and I had things to do. I had no intention, however curious I was, of taking a years-long detour into the land of faeries.

Still, today, I opened the window wide and went defenselessly back to bed. I knew it was dangerous, but I did it anyway.

The Varied Thrush is one of the quintessential Northwest forest birds. Though you might find one east of the mountains, or at the dry leafy base of a California madrone, the darkish, wet forests of the Northwest coast are the Varied Thrush's truest, favored home. The bird is often compared to another thrush, the American Robin of our backyards. "A robin with a black crescent across the breast," the beginner's guidebook instructs. This is only a starting point. Within the thrush family, the robin is placed, taxonomically, in a different genus than the Varied Thrush, and aside from their orange bellies and dark backs, the birds are only superficially comparable. The Varied Thrush is larger and stands more upright. If it is a brilliant male, the Varied Thrush has a slate blue back with a bright pumpkin-colored breast. The crescent on the breast and wide stripe across the eye are the darkest navy, and blue wings are vividly striped with orange. The female's breast is the same pumpkin-orange, paled by an undercurrent of yellow, and her back is leafy brown. Male or female, the Varied Thrush is a bird that literally startles with its vivid beauty.

Compared to the robins tromping boldly about our spring lawns, the Varied Thrush expresses a certain wariness. One ornithologist writes that the Varied Thrush exhibits a "furtive or scared look." But this is not quite right. I have never seen a bird so self-possessed as a Varied Thrush in the forest. I think the "furtive" look comes from a heightened awareness practiced by the bird when it ventures beyond the security of its home in the woodland depths. Outside of the forest, the thrush's steps are marked by a hesitating grace.

"If alarmed," this ornithologist continues, "it remains motionless, melting into its shaded background with remarkable effectiveness." I do agree with this. The thrush can disappear into the forest, blend in with a kind of magic that is rare and difficult to capture. This forest blending is true both in stillness and in flight. The motionless Varied Thrush disappears into a backdrop of decaying redcedar or, with a keen and practiced forest flight, rushes into the trees with an accipiter-like wing beat that might send a grasslands bird, or even a robin, headlong and broken-necked into the nearest ancient Sitka spruce.

The Varied Thrush is also quite different from the

other woodland thrushes that may be found in the Northwest, or anywhere else on the continent. These birds, the Veery, Swainson's Thrush, Wood Thrush, and Hermit Thrush, are all varying shades of forest-damp with spotted buffy breasts, altogether quite brown and subtly plumed, nothing like the vivid orange of the Varied Thrush.

All of these birds have thrush songs that are flutelike and melodious, inspiring impassioned prose to drip from the pens of their writerly observers. "This bird speaks to me out of an ether purer than that I breathe, of immortal beauty and vigor," writes Thoreau of the Wood Thrush he hears on his daily walk about Walden. On the surface, the Varied Thrush song is so much simpler. Instead of the bubbling chorus of notes and slurs characteristic of the other woodland thrushes, it is a single drawn-out note. It seems a note, rather, until you listen further and find that it is a chord, a harmonic layering of at least two different notes. The chord sings its way into the forest, then there is a rest—not quite silence—as the song stretches out, and hangs in the air, and is quiet. Just in the moment that one might think the song is spent, another chord is brought forth—and this at an irrational interval, slightly higher or perhaps lower than the last. I say irrational, but I actually do not know whether this interval is some thrush whim, thrush logic, thrush imperative, or thrush happenstance.

In spite of its surface simplicity, the song of the Varied

Thrush is described in the ornithological literature of the past century, over and over again, as the most remarkable bird song that the given writer has ever heard. In his 1940 *Birds of Washington*, Stanley Jewett rambles along in an appreciative but prosaic description of the bird, then alights with a hush upon the song, "a remarkable utterance, a trill which possesses a mysterious and faraway quality making it unlike any other bird's song. . . . Frequently several birds sing in company . . . a concert of voices both tender and plaintive and altogether charming and harmonious."

William Leon Dawson, the most elegant, flamboyant, effusive, and wonderful chronicler of Northwest birds, truly their Bard, surpasses even himself in a three-page rhapsody penned in 1909: "The thrush mounts the chancel of some fir tree and utters at intervals a single long-drawn note of brooding melancholy and exalted beauty—a voice stranger than the sound of any instrument, a waif echo stranding on the shores of time." Still, he cannot stop himself. "There is no sound of the western woods more subtle, more mysterious, more thrilling withal, than this passion song of the Varied Thrush. Somber depths, dripping foliage, and the distant gurgling of dark brown waters are its fitting accompaniments; but it serves somehow to call up before the mind's eye the unscaled heights and the untried deeps of experience."

The poetry is not diminished when we understand the physical modifications, remarkable in themselves, that allow such thrushlike song. Rather than a larynx—the human (and mammalian) "voice box"—birds vocalize using a syrinx, the muscular structure at the base of the avian esophagus. Air is moved through the syrinx, and brushes a layer of tissue called the tympanic membrane. Both extrinsic and intrinsic muscles combine to arrange the movement of air about this membrane and create the various avian vocalizations, including very complex songs.

For many birds, these muscles and membranes are very simple, or even lacking, and vocalizations are limited: pelicans, vultures, storks. Many birds can create interesting sounds, but cannot actually produce what is typically understood to be birdsong: doves, owls, shorebirds. The passerine species have the most advanced song–producing apparatus and, to the human ear, the loveliest vocalizations. Among the passerines, thrushes pull out the stops. Species in the group have two or more tympanic membranes that they can control individually with a particularly delicate set of syringeal muscles, thus producing layers of notes, actual chords, that boggle our minds and stop us in our tracks.

Though all the woodland thrushes share this physical ability to layer notes, no others pare their song to the strict simplicity of the Varied Thrush, whose entire strain is composed of a single, round chord. And though the showier, flutelike melodies of the other thrushes can be quite inspiring ("All is divine," chants Thoreau upon hearing a Wood Thrush), there is something about the

Varied Thrush's chord that strikes the listener with unknowable force. The song enchants.

Dawson makes much of the fact that the Varied Thrush is a particular lover of the Northwest damp. "Let the sun once veil his splendors," writes the Bard, "let the clouds shed their gentle tears of self-pity, let the benison of the rain-drops filter thru the forest, and let the leafage begin to utter that myriad soft sigh which is dearer than silence, and our poet Thrush wakes up." Varied Thrushes sing in the rain. When other birds hide fluffed and quiet under dripping branches, the male thrush perches atop the red, rotting stump of an ancient cedar, and sings. While other bird songs simply sound rained-on or muffled in wet, foggy conditions, the Varied Thrush song is given a body, and a kind of aural luminosity. Pumpkin underbelly shining out of human sight, the Varied Thrush sings a song that carries above the forest floor, through the trees, the fog, the rain. The ventriloquist voice finds its way far from the sender, rounding the trees to enter the tent, the sleeping bag at the river's edge, the open bedroom window, the sleeper's ear.

This kind of movement, this airborne travel and power of enchantment, is singular; the kind of listening it inspires has become increasingly rare. It seems the faeries of Varied Thrush legend know this, and they are not afraid to use the slight lull in our typically overactive psyches for their own purposes.

I will admit to feeling somehow brave today, speaking

of faeries with my eyes open, and without attempting a stylish edge of irony to make it sound as though I am writing with a slight smirk on my face. We are mature, millennial people, and faeries, in the common mind, are cute, greeting card fare. And there is no deadlier adjective here at the turn of the century. To be cute is to be, at least, uninteresting, certainly not fashionable, probably annoying. I am not into cute myself. But some of us already know that the faery world is anything but cute.

What I know of faeries I learned by studying the poet William Butler Yeats. Yeats was conversant with the idea of faeries, and with those who knew the beings themselves. He was a wannabe, if not an actual initiate, into their land and ways. In researching his book *Irish Fairy Tales,* Yeats uncovered some noteworthy facts: the great peasant-poet Carolan gathered his tunes while sleeping on a faery rath; faeries have a rather bad habit of stealing unattended children; if faeries injure someone (which is rare), it is usually well deserved (two people were actually killed for intentionally trampling the faeries' thornbushes); a young woman was taken to the faery realm and returned with no toes, for she had danced them off.

The Irish faeries that Yeats knew might take hapless humans as initiates into their great terrain of the imagination, the faeries themselves being envoys between the mortal and invisible worlds. Yeats believed in such a land as a true substrate to human being, and for him, the burden of disbelief was on the unbeliever.

After you return from a stint in the faery realm, your memories of the enchantment are erased, but the shift in consciousness is yours to keep, as is your new and radiant countenance, the occasional sweet lost remembrances and half-visions, the faerie intrusions into dreams and nightmares, the peculiar earthy intelligence, the uncanny attunement to the migrations of birds.

And while it is true that you may be away for a very long time if taken by the faeries, the thinking of my youth, the feeling of worry over lost time, was misguided. Because when you return, no time will have passed in the human realm. You get to be faerie queen for an eon, drinking wine from a mushroom cup, and still be home for dinner.

That doesn't sound so bad. I open my window to the Varied Thrush song and go back to bed—defenseless, but also eager. Too eager, I suppose, for the kind of listening that might allow a movement between worlds. But I am still hoping that one day I will get the balance right. That I might be possessed of the enchantment and vision that allows us to step meaningfully beyond everyday human boundaries and into the natural wild world, that allows this world to inform our own daily lives. It is this ongoing link that will redeem both of these interconnected worlds, that will permit them to continue with any kind of beauty and meaning.

What better envoy to a purer sense of vision than a

dripping, supernatural bird with a floating voice? A bird that visits us in a place where the stilted daily edges of our minds are softened by fog, a bird with a voice made palpable by the elements, a song that falls, with the mist, onto our hair. Our human role is to allow such a perfect elegance, to possess an unusual measure of courage, to listen, and to go.

Cormorant

Cormorant Problem

FIELD NOTES: Cormorants are not black, though they certainly seem so from a distance, and are reported as black in many texts. Through my scope I can see the individual feathers of the adult bird perched on the pier, lifting and separated in the wind. Each feather is gray–brown, outlined neatly in an iridescent black that is sometimes green, sometimes purple.

In the 1930s, an amateur naturalist fraternity, called the Linnaean Society, formed in New York. At that time, now-famous Harvard biologist Ernst Mayr was a young man, recently arrived in the United States from Berlin. He was disappointed by the society's focus on what he considered to be mundane detail—lists of local birds, early and late dates for the appearance and departure of migrants, the occasional sighting and identification of rarities. At that time Americans paid little attention to the life histories of birds, which so motivated the European ornithological societies.

Mayr became a mentor for many promising young men with an interest in birds. He urged them to pick a bird, to follow and study it, to learn the secrets of its breeding life, its winter habits, to take in small details that no one else knew because no one else had ever watched so closely. Mayr argued against a stream of ornithologists who hoped to make the science entirely academic, feeling that serious amateurs could make valuable contributions to the field of ornithology if they watched birds seriously and well. *Have a problem, everyone should have a problem.* This was the incantation with which Mayr filled his students' minds. It is largely due to Mayr's influence that competent amateurs today play such an important part in modern bird study.

Being a fan of Ernst Mayr's life history, I have tried to take his admonition to heart for the last two decades of my life, to always keep an avian problem in mind as an axis about which to wind my study and observation. With Mayr's voice in my head I have, over the years, spent hundreds of hours observing the courtship behavior of a small falcon, the Merlin, the foraging methods of the Red-eyed Vireo, the nesting habits of the Pigeon Guillemot, and the riverine existence of Harlequin Ducks on the Olympic Peninsula. I've watched birds in forests, at a distance, on rocky shores. And I learned more about these species from thorough and direct observation than I could ever have gleaned from bookish study.

Then I had a baby. I know other bird people with babies. Some of them strap the baby on their backs, fill their own pockets full of sippy cups and creamed sweet potatoes, and take to the road as if nothing had changed. They stray off-trail into dense forests in pursuit of Northern Pygmy-Owls, or wade the coastal shores through biting winds when a Bristle-thighed Curlew shows up on the Washington coast for the first time ever, never minding the runny-nosed little bundle all wrapped in polar fleece. A little rain never melted a baby, they say. As happy as I am to involve my daughter in naturalist pursuits of various kinds, I think these people are insane. I have domestic tendencies that keep me nearer to the warm and dry these days. Now I need a Mayr-ian problem that I can find closer to home.

After a few "problem-less" months spent getting accustomed to being a mom in the first place, I settled in to find one. Before Claire was born, I had always picked a bird that struck me for its particular beauty, its unique habits, or one that I had observed doing some strange birdish thing that made me curious. Now I needed a bird that fit certain mundane criteria: it had to be local, easy and reliable to find, and readily observable with an infant in tow.

I pulled out a notepad one rainy afternoon and listed the possibilities. I didn't want some flitty backyard bird, since I wanted to keep in some routine of bird-finding, even if it wasn't as far-flung as in my previous life. That eliminated all the feeder birds—no chickadees, Steller's Jays, crows, robins, finches, or flickers. I wanted something I would be likely to find within twenty minutes of my house just about any day of the year. That eliminated all the migrants. A species that would take advantage of my love of salt water and proximity to it would be ideal, but with migrants off the list, some of the best waterbirds were excluded—the pretty winter Mew Gulls, the Horned, Red-necked, and Western Grebes, even the various sea ducks that seem so common but disappear each spring to nest on the arctic tundra. After taking a variety of other factors into account, such as whether or not the various species or their close relatives had already been deeply studied by a popular author or a friend in the Northwest birding community, I settled, reluctantly, on the Double-crested Cormorant. It was the only bird left.

Why reluctantly? There was no good reason. The cormorant was one of the first birds that my husband learned to identify when we started dating. He still calls them "friends." Having spent a great deal of time on the

Olympic Peninsula, and living so close to Puget Sound, I've been in the near-constant presence of cormorants for years. Still, I've developed no particular interest in these tall, dark birds that eat fish and stand around with outspread wings. But the process had spoken. The Double-crested Cormorant was my bird, my problem. I intended to ascertain all that I could through simple but thorough observation, to learn something that, in spite of this being one of the most well-studied species in North America, no one else had seen.

That night, I carried a huge stack of books from my study to the living room coffee table, and curled up with a cup of tea, seeking inspiration. Some of my favorite ornithological writers were sure to have seen something beautiful or noble or at least terribly interesting in the cormorant, something that I had missed so far, some tidbit that would lend a spark of enthusiasm to my coming cormorant observations. I flipped through more than twenty volumes, exhausting my home library on the subject of Double-crested Cormorants. At the end of it I was inspired, but not at all in the manner I had imagined. As it turned out, no one had anything particularly nice to say about the Double-crested Cormorant.

Most early authors, while not writing anything forthrightly *mean* about the cormorant, commented noncommittally upon the natural history of the species, refraining from their usual lapses into wonder or poetry. Certainly not what I'd hoped for. So I turned to my ace-in-the-hole, my wild and word-loose Bard, William Leon Dawson. He managed to muster something about the Double-crested Cormorant's "handsome" blue-green eye, and its "sleek shininess." But then he turned to the subject of the cormorant rookery, their colonial nests upon rocky Pacific outcroppings. "Foul from every conceivable source," wrote the Bard, with young that are, if possible, "uglier than Magpies." The nestlings are "coal black and naked as sin, but their heads are scarcely larger around than their long necks, and a nestful of them looks more like a bundle of young black-snakes than anything avian."

References to the reptilian appearance of the cormorant—both young and adults—are common in the literature. Of course, birds are related to reptiles, and all avian young have a particularly reptilian aspect, especially the naked nestlings, with their scaly legs sticking out. But cormorants seem to go a step further in most observers' minds. John James Audubon wrote about the exploration of a cormorant rookery: "When the men approached [the young cormorants], they opened their bills, squeaked, hissed, and puffed in a most outrageous manner; and the noise produced by the multitudes on the island was not merely disagreeable, but really shocking." I can't help but think that he was overreacting. They "muted so profusely as to excite disgust." Disgust? They were just baby cormorants. Audubon continued, "I have never eaten cormorant's flesh, and intend to refrain from tasting it until nothing better can be procured."

This avowed by a man who, judging from his journals, was willing to eat *anything*.

So that was it. My every shred of human sympathy was aroused. No one loved the cormorant. Surely these insensitive, unthinking observers (a group of which I had, until this moment, been a core member) were missing something. I would find out what.

There are three species of cormorants common in the Pacific Northwest. The Brandt's and Pelagic Cormorants are strictly coastal, but the Double-crested Cormorant can be found inland, not only across the state, but throughout the country's wide interior. Cormorants are easily viewed from saltwater shores, but they also frequent freshwater lakes, reservoirs, wide rivers, and even smaller bodies of very urban water—the sort of lakes that are often surrounded by asphalt walking paths.

I have begun my own cormorant-watching in earnest. Frequenting the saltwater beaches near my home, I bring a spotting scope and binoculars, a warm drink, a stopwatch and notebook, and something soft to put between myself and my cold rocky perch. I open waterproof pages and begin to draw, tracing the arc of the cormorant neck, kinked in the middle, the back angling smoothly toward the water. In notes spidering off my sketches, I print physical details of the birds before me.

Three young birds spaced on piers, others passing in flight. Near bird: feathers very worn—throat and breast particularly mottled and dark, giving "smudged" impression. Top of bill is dark black and deeply scratched. Good size, thick head and neck, probably male.

Large, blackish, iridescent birds with orange bills and facial skin, Double-crested Cormorants are named for the two white crests that adorn their heads briefly during the courtship season. It is early spring, and the birds I am watching are not yet crested. Many are first-year birds, distinguished by their overall browner color and buffy necks and breasts. Male and female cormorants share identical plumage and are difficult to tell apart, though males may be slightly larger with a thicker head, neck, and bill. These differences are slim and subjective, and I am reluctant to assume the sex of a bird unless it seems remarkably large or slender. The adults all look alike to me, but the patterns of brown and light vary somewhat on the young birds, allowing me to tease out a few individuals and recognize some of the same birds from day to day, based on my sketches.

Still so young, this small juvenile with the spotted belly, the same I watched yesterday, possesses a graceful dive. Wings gently lifted at the shoulder, slightly extended as her body breaks the surface. Her dive is loon-like, splashless: head, followed by breast, back, and tail, partly spread. A gentle arc. Against all common sense, these birds look up and around between dives, not down into the water.

I watch for hours at a time, as individual cormorants arrive and depart. In flight, cormorants are competent, though not elegant, their rapid wing beats carrying them low over the water. Lighting on its surface, their bodies all but disappear, their snake-necks stretch above the water, their bills tilt up. They dive, and surface, over and over, before climbing, with a flap of their wings, and sometimes with difficulty, upon a floating log or pier or buoy, shaking their feathers and spreading their wings.

To void, stands firmly on perch, leans forward, body nearly horizontal, head and neck extended. Impressive white stream lands 2+ feet behind. Swirls on water's surface, disappears.

Cormorants dive for fish, and although they have occasionally been observed ingesting invertebrate fare, it is safe to call them near-exclusive fish-eaters. I cannot always tell whether a particular dive was successful, as the catch is sometimes swallowed before the bird surfaces, though often there is a silvery flash in the bill of a rising bird. Timing their dives, I have found that the cormorants in these near-shore, salt waters usually submerge for twenty to thirty seconds. One bird I timed for seventeen consecutive dives stayed under, according to my digital stopwatch, for exactly 30.12 seconds each and every dive. I started to think that I was making some strange mistake, or that my watch was broken, or that I was on *Candid Camera.* I've never seen another individual dive with such consistent precision. Double-crested Cormorants can dive, I have read, up to seventy meters, though some researchers suggest a more conservative thirty meters, still a substantial distance; and their bodies are entirely arranged about this life of water and depth and fish.

Like their close relatives the pelicans and darters, cormorants are totipalmate birds—all four of their toes are joined by webbing, rather than just the front three, as we are accustomed to seeing in other web-footeds, such as ducks and gulls. While diving they are propelled solely by their feet, and the totipalmate condition allows them to make the most of underwater resistance.

The external nostrils of cormorants are closed over by skin to keep water out of the nasal cavity during extended dives. The Double-crested Cormorant's eyes are not large, but the cornea is extremely thick and flattened, which may influence its light-refraction capacities in dark waters, and the muscles about the iris are unusually well developed, able to change the shape of the lens to further accommodate underwater vision. The bones of the rib cage are particularly thick and strong, able to withstand the pressures of deep-water dives upon the cormorant's body. And where most birds' bones are hollow or "pneumatic" to facilitate flight, the cormorant's are partly nonpneumatic, making them less buoyant and allowing longer dives with diminished effort. This heaviness is part of the reason cormorants ride so low upon the water's surface.

These are all important adaptations, but they are mostly invisible to the field observer. The obvious cormorant behavior, the one that sets them apart in all casual watchers' minds, is the spread-wing posture. After time spent foraging on the water, Double-crested Cormorants will clamber onto a low roost and widely spread their shining black wings. A striking, unforgettable pose, it is one of the most misunderstood avian activities in the popular study of birds.

Nearly every guidebook suggests that this is something cormorants—all cormorant species—do. Cormorants spread their wings to dry. I always took this as a given, until Dr. Dennis Paulson of the University of Puget Sound pointed out to me that it's simply untrue. Worldwide, many species of cormorants habitually wing-spread, some occasionally, some never. Here in the Pacific Northwest, the Double-crested is the wing-spreader; the smaller shag, or Pelagic Cormorant, spreads its wings sometimes; and the Brandt's Cormorant, another larger bird, almost never strikes the pose. Although students of Paulson's have worked on the question, the reasons for the differences between species regarding this behavior remain unclear. Just as interesting to me is that this difference has been so routinely overlooked in the literature. It is a dramatic and obvious distinction, useful in identification, as well as a puzzling ornithological question. Why is it so little known?

Passed down through generations of students is another persistent ornithological myth regarding the wing-spread posture of cormorants. I find it in my own twelve-year-old notes from "Biology 301: Ornithology": *The cormorant has no oil gland, so cannot waterproof its wings, and must spread them to dry.* Tom, Claire, and I recently took a chartered boat trip through the Kenai Fjords in Alaska with a tour group that emphasized natural history. There it was, the exact same line, in the colorful brochure provided as an introduction to the species we would encounter on our venture: *The cormorant has no oil gland. . . .* The naturalist on board told me that the information in the brochure was reviewed by biologists at the excellent marine research center in Seward.

Birds possess, at the base of their tails, a uropygial gland, sometimes called the "preen" or "oil" gland. When rubbed, it emits a protective oil that birds spend much of their day spreading over their feathers. This is what birds are doing when you see them rubbing their bills around the base of their tails. The oil keeps the feathers supple and healthy, and in some cases helps to insulate the birds by providing a measure of waterproofing. Watch a little longer, and you will see them carefully work the oil through their feathers, concentrating particularly on the long flight feathers of the wing, which they will often run through their bills one at a time. Frequently, when birds appear to be scratching the backs of their heads with their feet, they are preening areas that cannot be reached by the bill.

This supposed lack of cormorant oil glands was presented somewhat derisively by the instructor of my long-ago ornithology class. Here was a waterbird that couldn't waterproof its wings. The implication was that the cormorant was too primitive a bird, not sufficiently evolved to display the latest in proper avian adaptation. This was all in line with its prehistoric, reptilian appearance.

In truth, cormorants have finely functioning uropygial glands. If they didn't, their feathers would likely fall into early disrepair, with such constant exposure to the harsh elements of cormorant existence—salt water, cold, wind, sun.

Yet there is some truth to be untangled from the myth. Cormorant feathers are not particularly waterproof, but this is a further adaptation for a life that wends about watery depths. Most flying birds have feathers that zip together tightly, tiny barbules and hooklets that interlock to provide a barrier to water and other elements. When you look at cormorant feathers under magnification, you can see that the microarchitecture of their feathers is different: the barbules are spaced farther apart, and they hook together less readily, allowing water to collect on the spaces between, giving cormorants "wettable" feathers. The advantage is clear. The weight of the bird is increased, giving it less buoyancy, and more ease in deep dives.

So yes, many cormorants hold their wings out to dry, probably to ready their wings for flight, and possibly for thermoregulatory purposes as well. But the fact that cormorants have wettable feathers is not an example of their primitive nature. It is, rather, a complex adaptation to a diving, fishing life, a life that the cormorant has slipped into with an overt, stylish perfection. And while it is the sort of perfection that may be radically misunderstood, it is not the sort that goes unnoticed.

In China, people formed fishing partnerships with cormorants over two thousand years ago, as early as 317

B.C.E. The species used has always been the Great Cormorant, a close relative of the Double-crested, and one that is distributed across the earth, including parts of Europe, Africa, India, Australia, Tasmania, and New Zealand, as well as Japan and China. Cormorant nestlings in China are raised by hand, and at the age of four months, their training begins. Young cormorants learn to respond to the voice and whistled commands of their master. When they are ready to begin fishing, rings are fashioned about their necks that prevent them from swallowing larger fish; these also serve as attachment points for the leads that tether them to their boats or rafts.

During their training, some cormorants are allowed to eat every eighth fish as a reward, and often, after turning seven fish over to their human partner, they refuse to dive until their neck rings are removed. Amazingly, this suggests that cormorants can count, at least as high as seven.

Fishermen use a long bamboo pole to propel the boat, slapping it against the water as a signal to the cormorants that it is time to dive, and holding it out to the birds so that they can climb up on the pole as a perch to be carried back to the boat. The fish are removed by hand or disgorged by the birds directly into baskets held out by the fishermen. Fish small enough to pass through the neck ring are swallowed by the cormorants; when a bird is finished working, the ring is removed, and it is allowed to feed on larger fish as it pleases.

Typically, the cormorants are treated with care and

patience. In a recent radio interview, traditional fishing practices from the river Li in China's southern Guangxi region were considered. A translator spoke for Won Jin Tsigh, who, like his grandfather and great-grandfather, had spent his life on the water with Great Cormorants. "I treat these birds like they are my own brothers. Sometimes they get moody and bite, but I still feed them. I buy them good things to eat, like duck meat and honey." When the birds become too old to fish, Won Jin Tsigh buys them quantities of expensive delicacies, such as rice wine and dog meat. The birds are encouraged to eat all they want, and die from gorging upon too much wine and flesh.

The current generation of Chinese cormorant fishermen is probably the last, except for a few who will persist as cultural examples and sights for tourists. The rivers are so polluted that few fish remain.

In spite of this long and uniquely harmonious fishing partnership with birds in China, cormorants today are persistently vilified in the United States by people who catch fish commercially or for sport. While the Double-crested Cormorant is an ancient bird with a unique and quirky natural history and secrets to tell, much of the current research has focused on the human–cormorant conflict rather than topics of purely ornithological interest.

The conflict has many guises, but here in the Northwest it involves the perception that cormorants eat a disproportionate number of salmonid hatchery smolt in coastal estuaries and bays, contributing to dwindling numbers of various species' runs. Sport and commercial fishermen press wildlife and other government officials for permits to allow harassment or outright killing of cormorants to decrease the perceived impact of the birds, and to reserve consumption of the fish for human purposes.

In thirteen states, none of them on the West Coast, the Fish and Wildlife Service has issued depredation orders to aquaculturists, allowing them to kill as many cormorants as they see fit. The only requirement is that they report the number of dead cormorants to the service.

On the Great Lakes earlier in this century, cormorants almost completely died out as a result of chemical pollution of the waters, a problem that doubtlessly affected fish numbers as well. Now, as cormorant numbers recover, anglers blame decreased catches of smallmouth bass on the birds. Cormorants are *hated*. In one popular anti-cormorant treatise, the bird is blamed for its very existence: "A war is being waged between the interests of sport fishermen and a predatory bird that has no local natural enemy. The bird's sole purpose is to reproduce and eat fish." Of course, obtaining food and reproducing are two primary goals of any species, including our own.

In August 1998, nearly one thousand cormorants were found illegally slaughtered by gunshot on Little Galloo island in eastern Lake Ontario. Evidently, the Fish and Wildlife Service took too long in its review of the situation and was not stridently anti-cormorant enough to suit the perpetuator of the crime. Many birds flew away as the shooting began on the densely populated island rookery. Many of the birds killed were young, unable to fly. Many were nestlings, left parentless to die from exposure and starvation. And many hundreds were injured, neither entirely alive nor quite dead.

Naturally, the factors that contribute to dwindling fish numbers extend beyond cormorant fishing. Most of them are human-caused, including water pollution, overfishing, and dams. Here in the Pacific Northwest, it is entirely unclear whether cormorants have any significant negative impact on salmonid numbers. They may even improve salmon populations in the long term by culling sick or weakened fish, thereby strengthening the gene pool. Hatchery smolt are extremely naive and unwary of predators. Some suggest that exposure to fish-eating animals such as cormorants can "teach" the smolt to avoid predators as they grow. Most important, even when cormorants are seen feeding near schools of salmonid smolt, it is unlikely that they are eating only salmon. They are perhaps eating fish that prey on salmon, at least in part, so reducing cormorant numbers could actually increase the impact of other, more effective salmon predators. In years when cormorant harassment was allowed on the Oregon coast, salmon returns did not improve.

In 1909 William Leon Dawson wrote of the Double-crested Cormorant, "The piscatorial peculations of men are as a dot beside their unceasing pillage, yet we do not begrudge the cormorants the exercise of their ancient rights." The numbers of fish taken by cormorants now pale beside those taken by commercial gill-net fisheries, and yet we still begrudge their "ancient rights" in deep earnest. With all the non-cormorant factors that affect fisheries, it is curious that we focus so darkly on a bird that has evolved alongside ocean fishes since the early Eocene, 55 million years ago. Besides humans, many other animals consume salmonids, including marine mammals such as harbor seals and sea lions, and birds like kingfishers, mergansers, herons, and loons. And while fishermen are none too fond of any of these animals, the cormorant seems a locus for the most emotional of human sentiments.

Writing *Paradise Lost* in 1667, that John Milton had likely never viewed a cormorant colony, though he may have seen individual birds perched in trees. Still, we have this from his imagined travels of Satan: *Thence up he flew, and on the Tree of Life / The middle tree and highest there that grew / Sat like a Cormorant.* . . . The depth of the human response to the bird suggests a source beneath the surface of rationality. Is it the neck that, at certain angles, moves like a snake? The large darkness of the bird, like a shadow, that some unfamiliar part of us cannot help but distrust? It seems that the bird's simple color may, in part, invoke our suspicion. Crows and ravens, other large, black birds, often invite this same response. The name cormorant combines the Latin *corm*, crow, with *marinus*, of the sea.

I am still at the beginning of my Double-crested

Cormorant studies. Frequenting the Puget Sound beaches near my home, I laugh at myself as, scanning the waters, I overlook less common and more traditionally interesting birds, whispering "*There's one*" when the cormorant silhouette appears, a shadow I would barely register in my pre-cormorant days. How readily the intimacy of close observation replaces indifference with affection. I try to watch several hours a week, at least, and though I admit that I don't know quite what I am watching *for,* I cannot yet fathom all that there is to see. A close and present bird, the cormorant is eagerly misunderstood by fishermen and ornithologists alike.

Cormorants in high wind. Five birds struggle for balance as their log–piling perches pitch strongly in the wind. The birds sit facing the wind, bodies bent forward. All are positioned at the edge of the log, which they clutch with large feet, wrapping at least half of their webbing over the ledge, grasping with curved black toenails. Gulls perched nearby look perfectly graceful and balanced in comparison, resting easily in the center of their perch. The cormorant's fourth toe is attached to the others by webs—maybe it is easier for gulls, with one toe fully facing the rear, and a rounder, compact body. Still, the cormorant silhouette is more intricate, poised in its own way. Even with all this motion, I can see the shining sea–green eyes, exactly round.

These birds are not "above" the human fray that surrounds them, but simply, as individual beings, entirely apart from it. I see that a cormorant is always perfect.

A young cormorant, fishing, is joined by another. They dip their heads, dip them again, then shake the water from their shimmering feather coats. The birds dip once more and, in a gesture I have never seen described in the literature, greet one another, bodies facing, cheek to cheek.

The Birdwatcher's Book of Secrets

One of my favorite books about birds is a thick, black 700-page tome titled *Identification Guide to North American Birds, Part I,* by Peter Pyle. It lacks narrative interest, color plates, and sometimes even complete sentences. But it is a dreambook, full of bird poetry, avian knowledge, and mystery. And though it's a favorite, I had to check the spine to get the title right, because I usually call it by my own name, one of endearment as well as description—*The Birdwatcher's Book of Secrets.*

The book has a subtitle. *A compendium of information on identifying, aging and sexing near-passerines and passerines in the hand.* Passerines are the typically small, perching birds we think of as "songbirds." The taxonomically close but not-quite-passerines, or "near-passerines" as Pyle calls them, include the doves, woodpeckers, kingfishers, hummingbirds, swifts, cuckoos, owls, and nightjars. In practical terms, this is a manual for bird banders, patient people who research birds by catching them briefly to band and study them. They set up sails of thin, nearly invisible netting to arrest birds in flight. After gently disentangling a bird, banders ring one of its legs with a numbered silver band canonized by the Fish and Wildlife Service, then record bits of information about the bird before releasing it, ideally (though not always) none the worse for wear. The species of the bird is only the first of these information bits, and in fact Pyle's book pretty much assumes that you already know what kind of bird you are holding. Banders are also asked to weigh the bird and record its sex and age, the stage of feather wear and molt, the subspecies represented by the bird, any evidence of hybridization, the presence of external parasites, and whether or not the bird is in breeding condition. All of this, while most of us are standing around with the simplest of thoughts in our brains: "I think it's some kind of sparrow."

Pyle's book reveals all known details for determining more about an individual bird than just its species. While most of us are finished with a bird once we've identified

it, Pyle's book refuses to throw any single bird into a heap
bearing a species name. According to Pyle, the name is
just a starting point. Every turn of feather and curve of
bill has secrets to tell about a bird's entirely individual
identity.

Once they are a year old, male and female birds of
many passerine species look very much alike. The sexes
are indistinguishable by plumage characteristics observable in the field. If you see, say, a nice blue and black
Steller's Jay in your apple tree, you are unlikely to be able
to determine much about it, other than its species.
Sometimes young birds behave naively, and this can be a
clue, though an inconclusive one, to general age. But
reading Pyle's account of the Steller's Jay, I learn that the
age of young jays can be determined by opening the bill
and checking the amount of white on the inside roof of
the mouth. A preponderance of white indicates a juvenile, or hatch-year bird; white mottled with black is a
bird later in its hatching year or early in its second year;
and an all-black interior upper mandible indicates a full
adult, a bird that is likely in its second year at least.

Perhaps this is not the most useful of information for
the backyard ornithologist. But privately considering the
lining of the jay's upper mandible, knowing that the bird
holds this small secret, among thousands of others,
brings me a certain delight.

Pyle's book teaches that if I possess an innate flair for
the art, if I am schooled by a knowing mentor and practice

diligently, I might judge the age of any bird by slightly wetting its scalp and palpating its skull. I might divine the abundance of insects in a bird's diet by examining certain bars on the tail feathers. Or ascertain the sex of a bird by the length of its primary wing feathers, or identify it to subspecies by a tiny notch in one of these same feathers, or a particular cast of gray.

Certain small warblers can be aged and sexed by the patterns in the "median coverts," the tiny feathers that cover their wings. One of the Pacific Coast subspecies of the Savannah Sparrow can be distinguished by the depth of its nostrils. The age of Vesper Sparrows might be revealed through the shape of their outer tail feathers. In some woodpeckers, the sexes differ quite dramatically in the length of their tongue barbs. There are, I am guessing, tens of thousands of such facts in Pyle's book.

One flip through the deep detail, ambitious vocabulary, very small print, and enigmatic diagrams of Pyle's book reveals that it is not for the faint of heart. But maybe it is more for all of us than one might, at first glance, suppose.

Ostensibly, this is a book for bird banders, who really need the information to do their job, to track the movements and well-being of species and individuals and, ultimately, to apply this knowledge to conservation decisions. This purpose, in itself, has obvious import. But if I may say so, Pyle seems pleasingly and impractically crazed for all of this information, and for more.

In the book's introduction he apologizes to friends,

family, and colleagues for being so "elusive and unre-
laxed" during the book's recent revision. I picture him
bent over and tight-shouldered, dictating these details
into his beleaguered computer, relentless with the information. Have we seen something Pyle missed when he
amassed these details from the corners of the continent?
Well, for god's sake, write it down and send him a post-
card. He asks over and over. Look, look, look, Pyle's book
screams. No, better, *see*, then see some more. I shake my
head and wonder, "What manner of love is this?"

I suppose it might be argued that, for the amateur
watcher seeking a meaningful connection with birds, this
attention to remote detail is just another form of scientific reductionism, that harried foe of poetry and wonder. In my experience, it is so much the opposite. The
tinier the details I come to comprehend, the more bewil-
dered I become, the richer, it seems, the more inspiring
of awe, is the biological life I manage to encounter.

The minutiae offer a focus that bridges the aesthetic
and scientific worlds. We confront a simple, common
bird, the Black-capped Chickadee, maybe, and know that
165 million years of avian evolution coalesce here—on
this very particular notch on a single bird's seventh primary wing feather, on this peculiar discoloration of the
shaft. We are drawn smaller and farther down until our
bodies seem obese and clumsy when we stand up again.
Here is the movement of life.

I have banded only a few hundred birds in my life, a

mere beginner's beginning. And for reasons of my own I have sworn off banding. But I still keep Pyle's book on the night table, and make tiny advances into this strange collection of knowledge, absorbing details one by one into my brain, my poor little brain that remembers very few of these at all, and wonders, sometimes, what to do with the ones that it manages to keep. Pry open the bills of hapless Steller's Jays that alight in my apple tree and announce, triumphantly, their ages? I try to restrain myself.

But if we watch, I am quite sure that the details will start to coalesce, revealing a new kind of whole, a shift in knowledge (somewhat important) and awareness (much more so) of a detailed world. This realm is both material and tangible, and yet not entirely comprehensible, a twining of the rarefied and the everyday. At this meeting place even the most common bird holds riddles, right in the fold of its feathers. And mystery can be material, making even the most ordinary details a matter of the soul. And no matter how much information we have gleaned from the pages of Peter Pyle's brimming volume, this living bird before us is different still, crossing the sidewalk, watching and stepping, shrouded in secrets.

Northern Flicker

When Good Woodpeckers Go Bad

It's been over a year since I left my job at the Seattle Audubon Society. Still, it is full-fledged springtime, and I almost expect my home phone to start ringing off the hook, just as my office phone once did at this time of year. For a brief few weeks each spring, every other call to Seattle Audubon—and I am sure this is the case for other local chapters as well—is a woodpecker call, and somehow I became the organization's *de facto* one-woman wood-pecker-response team. Because I was the education coordinator, and this was considered a public education issue, most of the calls got funneled my way. All the callers had just one thing to say, and say loudly. "A woodpecker is destroying my house!"

I would give the caller some time to blow off steam before attempting to respond.

"Yes! Destroying it! Banging loudly and endlessly all day! Can't sleep! Can't chase it away!" And typically there was an implied, if not an overt, question. "What are you going to do about it?" As if it was altogether possible that I would pop over driving an Audubon Woodpecker Relief Mobile, and—and what? Reason with the bird, perhaps? Relocate him? Pull out my Audubon Society pellet gun and send him on the path to glory?

This last option was not always so far from the mind of the disgruntled home owner. From the little tally that I kept on a notepad, I counted that roughly one-quarter of the total springtime woodpecker callers asked whether they were "allowed" to shoot the bird themselves. Happily, the legal answer rested squarely on the side of woodpecker longevity.

It is true, though, that this time of year, woodpeckers go absolutely nuts. They are not alone. The male birds of many species are hit with a wild hormone boost, putting them in the mood for avian romance. They have two primary, closely related goals: to define and defend a territory, and to attract an excellent, willing mate. Noise is one of the best avenues to both ends.

For passerine species, the "songbirds," spring is the season for rhapsodizing ceaselessly from the highest branches. And though both male and female birds vocalize, it is the males that sing. I once heard folksinger Linda Waterfall translate the male's spring song: "I'm a hot date and a good provider! I'm a hot date and a good provider!" This is a workable rendering. The song has a dual audience—potential female mates and would-be marauding males. The angle on the song is somewhat fluid depending on the moment in the nesting cycle. Late in the season, presumably, the bird has already mated, and his song helps to maintain the pair bond and to reiterate territorial command.

Woodpeckers, however, aren't songbirds. They have ringing calls but are not memorable singers. In lieu of song, woodpeckers become astonishing, loud, and unforgettable in their own special way. Bills poised and ready, male and female woodpeckers begin a spring symphony of loud drumming, rap-rap-rapping their strong bills against anything that will produce the desired effect. Drumming posts are selected and used repeatedly during the season, the posts being chosen, it appears, for their instrumental quality and amplitude. A hollow tree is good, but not as good as your metal storm drain.

The Northern Flicker is the most oft-encountered

suburban woodpecker. Fawn-brown and black-spotted, flickers have dark, wide-set eyes and an inquisitive, dolphinlike expression. There are two forms of Northern Flicker, which were once considered separate species: the Yellow-shafted and Red-shafted Flickers, named according to the color of their wing linings. Eastern birds display yellow underwings in flight. Here in the West, they are orange-vermillion. In both cases, the colors glow.

The wings are the most obvious, but not the only, difference. William Leon Dawson was appalled upon overhearing easterners visiting the West referring to resident flickers by one of the colloquial names used for birds in their region. In his lovably high-minded style, Dawson writes in 1909, "Thoughtless people often call the Flickers of Washington 'Yellow-hammers,' quite regardless of the fact that the western Flicker is no longer yellow, but orange-red. Such an oversight is *unpardonable*." Beyond the underwing differences, the forms are further distinguished by the male's raindrop-shaped moustachial stripes—red in the Red-shafted, black on the Yellow-shafted. The eastern birds also have a bright red crescent on their napes. There is a stable hybrid zone in the United States, where nearly all birds seen are reliable integrations of red- and yellow-shafted birds.

The flicker's relationship to the suburban landscape is more complicated than it seems on the surface. Less dependent on purely forested habitat than many woodpeckers, flickers appear to adapt nicely to the suburban landscape. Open areas are necessary for optimal flicker foraging, a need well met by nicely planted residential lawns. But suburbs also remove much of the nesting substrate for these birds, which prefer to raise their young in natural cavities. In the neighborhoods, contact with starlings means increased competition for nest sites.

For the moment flickers are common, though it is not odd for the uninitiated to see flickers every day without even realizing that they are in the company of a woodpecker. Flickers are the most terrestrial of the North American woodpecker species. In a most unwoodpeckerly fashion, flickers will be seen walking across suburban backyards, much like a robin, seeking insect meals and favoring ants in particular. Flickers hang from tree trunks too, like good woodpeckers should, and they share all of the proper woodpecker adaptations for scaling trees and eating insects. Woodpeckers have two toes pointing forward and two back, for sure gripping of vertical trunks. They have pointed, stiffened tail feathers that are resistant to the wear received when used as props against a tree. They have astonishingly long tongues that wrap all the way around the back of their skulls, across their foreheads, and between their eye sockets, attaching at the top base of the bill. These tongues, also barbed and sticky, pick ants easily, and can be extended into holes the bird has excavated in search of insects or wood-boring grubs. Most important, woodpeckers have expanded brain cases, allowing for space and cushioning between the brain and the skull. If we humans rapped our bills against a tree with the force of a woodpecker, our brains would be liquefied in less than a minute.

The fact that Northern Flickers are common and readily observed will, ideally, only increase interest in these extraordinary, animated birds. Flickers have terrific personality. They call and yack, peer and hop, perform mating "dances" with much prehistoric wagging of the head, and tend to all manner of flicker details in the course of a busy day. And they don't mind if you watch.

A yellow-shafted bird is credited with inspiring one of the most famous careers in modern birding, a story the late Roger Tory Peterson loved to recount. As an angst-ridden young soul of twelve, Roger happened across a soft heap of dead-looking brown feathers, and when he reached for them, they burst forth in a wild fury of color and vitality. As he tells it, this was the most significant moment of his life, turning him toward a professional life built around birds.

Flickers are championship drummers. They will spend some time and effort seeking a post that produces the most possible noise, and will stick with the favored spot for the entire drumming season. Houses sided in aluminum are great. So are metal chimneys. And even houses that lack a great deal of metal might have gutters, or a nice thump to the cedar shakes.

But it is here that most recipients of woodpecker home-rapping attentions go awry in their thinking. Even if the bird is drumming on pure wood, it is highly unlikely that much destruction is going on. Sure, the flicker could peck your house to bits if it wanted to; it could bore your wood siding full of holes (and if a woodpecker is feeding from your house, then woodpeckers are the least of your problems—you probably have rotten wood and a termite infestation). But destruction is not the flicker's purpose. Your house is a noisemaker, most likely not a restaurant, and the behavior is, if not soothing, at least temporary.

If you are more worried about your own sleep than the reproductive success of the neighborhood woodpecker, here are some simple steps you can take. Most birds, woodpeckers included, avoid things like streamers moving in the breeze. You might hang a wind sock, or a plastic garbage bag cut into strips, near the bird's favored drumming site. You could also reduce your home's noise potential. Cover the drumming area with a temporary layer of foam. The need for aesthetically unappealing measures such as these will be short-lived, since by earliest summer the flickers will have no further use for your home. They will be too busy bringing food to their tiny, featherless, woodpecker young.

But it could surely be argued that these anti-woodpecker measures do not represent the higher ground. The flicker is dropping a singular opportunity in front of our faces, and if we keep our wits about us, we might take a step toward something more rare and wild than our everyday life typically affords. Untamed woodpeckers courting and mating on our simple rooftops. Here is much to learn.

Forget early morning sleep. Put off reading boring books that require noiseless concentration. After all, even the 1995 Space Shuttle Discovery mission was delayed several weeks by Yellow-shafted Flickers, which, in the throes of biological imperative, drummed six dozen small holes in the foam insulation of the Discovery's brownish red external fuel tank. Most of us don't even have a launching schedule. Why not relax and enjoy our part in the cycles of nature, resting happily in the knowledge that a cavity-nest filled with fluffy wood-pecker babies was helped into existence by the resonant capacities of our own domicile?

The family of freshly fledged woodpeckers will grace your yard later this summer. The only thing cuter than a flicker is a baby flicker. You can watch the parents non-chalantly demonstrate how to find ants most effectively, how to balance ear and eye. Soon the young will stand up straighter, you will be less able to tell them by their hunched postures and bad landings. These first-year birds will disperse, becoming wild things of their own, with adult lives. The young might practice a few taps in the fall—not mature drumming yet, nothing terribly impressive. But watch for them next spring. Next spring they'll be ready.

Pacific-slope Fly Catcher

The Pacific-slope Flycatcher: A New Species, Sort of

Beginning our day-hike in the lower west Cascades, Tom and I are greeted by the repetitive call of a Northern Pygmy-Owl, floating through the forest from who knows how far away. We see a brilliant Western Tanager, looking every bit the tropical bird that it is in yellow and black and red feathers, and then hear the familiar pee-sit! of the Pacific-slope Flycatcher.

"It used to be the Western Flycatcher," I mention to Tom, who is genuinely interested in such ornithological arcana, "until a couple of years ago when it was split, divided into two species, the Pacific-slope and the Cordilleran Flycatchers. "

"Is there still a Western?"

"Nope."

"Gone?"

"Into the ether."

Tom ponders a moment, then worries aloud, "I hope someone remembered to tell the birds."

We wonder what such a notification might look like. Surely this kind of action requires written notice. Perhaps a telegram?

Dear Resident Flycatcher:

As chair of the American Ornithologists Union's nomenclatural reform committee, it is incumbent upon me to inform you that based on recent genetic evidence and geographical variations in vocalizations we have no choice but to conclude that your previous species, Empidonax difficilis, *the Western Flycatcher (the moniker under which you have so long and prosperously dwelt), is in fact two separate species: the Pacific-slope Flycatcher, which will retain the scientific designation* E. difficilus, *and the Cordilleran Flycatcher, to be known hereafter in the scientific literature as* E. occidentalis. *We trust that you will be pleased with your new taxonomic status, and apologize for any confusion or inconvenience this may cause. Please post this notice.*

Would a flycatcher take time from her busy day to make note of such a sweeping reform? Regarding these nomenclatural goings-on, all the birds in my path have seemed decidedly uninterested. Not out of naiveté, I am certain, but more out of a transcendent attitude regarding such efforts. As long as our taxonomic structures are at least moderately accurate, we are, in the birds' eyes, free to label them as we see fit. Surely it is human business.

The American Ornithologists Union (AOU) codifies North American bird names in its "Checklist of North American Birds," appended and amended in a new edition every several years. When an updated checklist comes out, I pour myself a cup of tea and start crossing things out, adding things, and generally bringing my field guide up to speed with the current thinking. Tedious. And always I ask myself, "Why am I doing this?"

But I do know why.

Species designations are, in some ways, the most "real" form of taxonomic order that we impose in our naming of the natural world. Higher taxonomic divisions—the order, the family, the genus, all of these hierarchical dimensions of the taxonomic enterprise—are somewhat artificial human constructions that we use to organize and understand the natural world. Though they are designed to make sense given similarities and differences in groups of organisms, and though taxonomic structures at their best mimic true evolutionary relationships, in fact these distinctions have little bearing on an animal functioning in an ecological system.

Species, "natural kinds" as Aristotle insightfully named

them, are another matter. Taking birds as our example, it is clear that they are designed to look and sound like members of a specific group, and to recognize others in this group. Plumage, vocalization, and behavior all contrive to keep birds in their own species reproducing with their own kind, and mostly no others. Animals work within their own species strictures.

All first-year ecology students learn the functional "biological species definition." Animals in the same species can mate and produce viable offspring. This is usually true, though certain hybrids are viable, such as the common Glaucous-winged Gull and Western Gull crosses that populate the Pacific Coast. Modern genetic studies and deepening understanding of evolutionary relationships hone our sense of species delineation. Still, the biological definition is a mostly true and useful interpretation that follows the function of species in nature.

Before the Pacific-slope Flycatcher was granted full species status, it was, along with the Cordilleran Flycatcher, considered a subspecies of the Western. Subspecies are recognizable groups within species that are typically defined by geographic range. They are noted in the literature by a third scientific name attached to the usual two. There are thousands of subspecies floating around that are not mentioned in the field guides used by birdwatchers, and subspecies are not normally given their own common names. Shuffling of subspecies allows taxonomists to continue a kind of species-level ambiguity until they decidedly figure things out. It is, after all, a brave move to proclaim a new vertebrate species.

Our growing understanding of birds constantly changes our notion of how they should be grouped taxonomically. More than this, though, philosophies differ as to what constitutes a full species, as opposed to a subspecies. This leads to much debate, discussion, trauma, and scandal in ornithological circles. Some experts wish to "lump" groups of subspecies that show limited geographic variation under a single species name; others want to "split" single species into two or more species that seem to show a reasonable amount of differentiation, as was the case with the Western Flycatcher.

For taxonomists, lumping and splitting seems to come in waves of fashionability. When the AOU was formed in the early 1880s it went busily to work, rampantly splitting birds into ever-smaller specific and subspecific groupings, greatly annoying the amateur birdwatching contingent. Now, after a brief lumping phase only a decade or two long, the AOU seems to be back to a splitting free-for-all.

A bright yellow sticker graces the cover of the new *National Geographic Guide to the Birds of North America,* third edition, one of the guides preferred by "serious" birdwatchers. "80 New Species!" the sticker proclaims. New species! As if researchers have been out, in the decade since the second edition was published, finding fabulous and previously overlooked tiny birds in America's forest canopies, on isolated shores, or perhaps in the cleft red rocks of the

Utah desert. Ah, those were the days, when a new species was a new species. Imagine Lewis and Clark, describing birds new to an English-speaking population for the very first time. Such a dream. Of course, not a single one of the new species is truly new. The Rufous-sided Towhee is now the Spotted Towhee and the Eastern Towhee. The Scrub Jay is now the Island Scrub Jay, the Florida Scrub Jay, and the Western Scrub Jay. The Solitary Vireo is now the Plumbeous, the Cassin's, and the Blue-headed Vireo. And of course, there are our flycatchers.

More than a little controversy surrounds the split of the Western Flycatcher. It is based on genetic evidence reported in the late 1980s, but some feel that the research was insufficient to justify the ensuing split. In terms of observable physical features, this case is even muddier than most. Looking at the two flycatchers in your field guide, you might reasonably swear that the same color plate has been duplicated, with different names identifying the same image. The Pacific-slope and Cordilleran Flycatchers look like exactly the same bird. It is, in fact, pretty much impossible to tell these birds apart in the field based solely on physical appearance. We are directed to note their geographical location and listen for vocal variations to differentiate the species.

Even Peter Pyle, in his guide to identifying birds in the hand based on the tiniest minutiae, cautions us that these two flycatcher species may be indistinguishable. Pyle compares the colors of tiny flycatcher backs, breasts, and wing-bars, which might help us to tell the two species, and their subspecies, apart. This is the subtle palette that confronts the would-be identifier: olive, brightish olive, greenish olive, darker olive, brownish olive, dull olive. Buffy, dark buffy, buffy lemon, ocher-buff, buffy-to-white, dingy whitish with a yellow tinge, pale lemon, medium pale, dull whitish, brownish-white. We are provided with no color chart.

To further confuse things, ardent students of the flycatcher here in Washington have observed single individuals singing both of the songs that supposedly differentiate the two species, as well as songs intermediate between the two. They are at a loss to establish reliable geographical boundaries that might separate the species. These gifted amateur ornithologists are among the most vocal opponents of the controversial split.

Is the Western Flycatcher one species or two? Part of the confusion and difficulty in answering might lie in the fact that we are struggling to impose a static name—using a system little-changed since a century before Darwin—on a dynamic, fluid, evolutionary lineage. At the moment, the Western Flycatcher might be neither one definitive species nor two, but muddling its way, through the course of evolutionary change, in one direction or the other. It seems that in this case we have been drawn into a natural confusion, and the cries of "insufficient" evidence and intergradation of types are a more accurate reflection of the natural world than a decisive lump or split could be.

The birds appear to be comfortable living within this confusion, even as our own lexicon-driven minds are not.

Some people feel that the politics, power, codes, and obscure science involved in species naming are too esoteric to be of interest to folks who simply wish to observe, enjoy, and conserve the earthly birdlife. I have friends who are very pure in their appreciation of nature. They are "response-ists," finding emotional and spiritual sustenance in the natural world, eschewing the supposed hubris involved in naming and numbering all the innocent organisms, refusing to lessen a bird's innate worth by garnishing it with a human moniker. I find this annoying, just as the opposite view—that scientific understanding eclipses mystery or subjective passion—is annoying.

It would be arrogant to feel that our names somehow impart reality or validity to wild creatures. But they do give us a watery starting point for immersion and observation, for allowing birds into our human sphere and, so far as we can enter, us into theirs. I, for one, am happy that someone is looking as closely as possible and reporting back to me, in however stilted an academic tongue, what they have seen.

The Pacific-slope Flycatcher: here it is, on a moist Pacific slope, making just the distinctive call note that my guidebook leads me to expect. Not bad. And all this naming has taught me a great deal about the biological details that are at issue for this bird, today, in an evolutionary moment that has consequence and meaning, and reaches beyond itself into the future of this species, and so many others. In the changing details of our field guides, we offer the birds, at best, a veiled approximation of their reality. But it is our own human point of contact, our best effort, and it serves us well. The birds work out their own relationships, and so, in lagging time, we will come to understand them. In the meantime we point, and name, and gasp over beauty, and ponder confusions, and read from our books, over and over again. And if the birds do not forgive us our plodding intellect, they are, at least, kind enough to ignore it.

Blue Grouse

The Hidden Blue Grouse

It is difficult to know what to think of grouse. They have large eyes spaced widely on heads that are too small for their fat, oval bodies. They appear and, if I may say so, *behave* as if simple-minded. They seem a band of ruffled, twitching birds living in a perpetually nervous, vapid condition. I do try to appreciate grouse both aesthetically and biologically, but it is no use denying that I harbor a secret prejudice. Whenever I encounter a grouse of any kind, I stand poised with high purpose, ready to think kind and enlightened grouse thoughts. Then, notwith-standing my best intentions, just one judgment prevails. "Not too bright a thing, is it?"

In spite of my unjustified prejudice against the grouse mind and body, I enjoy finding and observing these avian curiosities just beyond my comprehension; there is something that nags at me to seek them out. Three species of forest grouse inhabit the western Washington landscape, and they fan out nicely along an elevational continuum. The Ruffed Grouse can be readily observed in lowland forests and edges, as soon as you get to the edge of town. In high subalpine forests the Spruce Grouse lives its strange fir-needle-eating life. And in the middle, sometimes overlapping the two species above and below, is my particular favorite, the Blue Grouse.

Unless you happen upon a displaying male bird, the Blue Grouse, like others of the grouse ilk, is inconspicuous, giving the impression of being somewhat less common than it actually is. Covered softly with sooty gray-blue feathers, and possessing wide, quiet feet atop which it roosts in the very crown of fir trees or walks with muffled steps upon decaying cedar soil, the bird is seldom seen. It is, more often, heard.

In early spring, knee-deep in snow, the male Blue Grouse commences hooting. *Hoot. Hoot. Hoot*. Low and hollow, with oddly spaced pauses between each effort. *Hoot. Hoot. Hoot*. The hooting of the male Blue Grouse, a tireless effort made for the sake of the Blue hen, carries far through the coastal forests, the voice transcending the grouse itself. For it happens that this slim-witted little bird, much to the consternation of its aspiring watchers, is a gifted ventriloquist.

This ventriloquism is one of the deep and curious blendings of the Blue Grouse and its woodland home. Most bird species go to some length to create a protected life in a given place: building hidden nests, actively guarding young, hunting food. Blue Grouse life is pared down to a spare simplicity. It eats conifer needles, seeds, berries, easily catchable insects, foods it just happens to be stepping over. Rarely bothering to fly, the grouse sits in trees and walks on earth, relying entirely on an ability to melt into the background of the landscape as protection against grouse marauders. If a grouse doesn't want to be seen or bothered, it doesn't leave, it simply holds very still.

This is particularly true of a female on her nest, flush with the earth. She has not hidden the nest particularly well, but rather constructed it out of the very materials with which the nest itself is surrounded—leaves, mosses, needles, lichens. On top of it, she looks like more of the same. Trusting utterly in her own invisibility, the hen will not move from her nest until an elk or bear or human is about to step right on top of it, at which juncture she will fly with a heart-stopping ruckus into the intruder's face. A warier watcher might crawl up and give the soft bird some gentle pats.

In my thinking, the perpetual hooting of the male is

another kind of blending, not as elegant as the female's nest-building and setting, but harmonious in its own way. It is not just the grouse's creation of the hoot itself, but the way that the hoots interact with the layered forest, that results in the ventriloquial effect. The grouse does his part by producing a very round baritone call. The forest picks up the sound and spreads it up and down its branches, across its mosses, nestles the tone in its ferns, throws it far, unthinned. The male grouse bellows from the rafters, and still cannot be found.

Birdwatchers know this, but do not learn. When you hear this hooting, a kind of grouse possession takes over. You must see the grouse, and why not spend a few minutes looking for it? It sounds so close. Off you go, scanning the treetops, rounding forested corners, checking the open mossy areas, closing in; you are sure it is just around the next fern, or orchid, or wet ring of morels. *Hoot. Hoot. Hoot.* An hour passes, and no grouse. But surely after all this time you are close! You cannot stop. Another hour. Blood sugar and morale are low. Head in your hands, optimism gone, the hooting mocks you. Which way is the trail? Your car? You hate the grouse.

There is nothing that can melt this feeling of ill will faster than the occasional hard-won sight of the male Blue Grouse, who is not simply hooting, but dancing a display ritual for the sake of the female (who, by the way, never has a difficult time tracking down the hoots). The red, fleshy combs above his eyes stand bright and erect.

His tail is stiff and fanned and lifted. The feathers on each side of his neck are spread most impressively into sheer white circles, revealing smooth, inflated, yellow air sacs. The bird walks in circles, much too engrossed to notice you. He is concentrating ridiculously on his simple steps.

And there it is again. Grouse prejudice. Is he not regal? Stunning and manly? Graceful, colorful, and brave? I try to think so. But all I can muster, besides the feeling of being very happy to be in the forest with a displaying Blue Grouse, is "ridiculous."

I take pains to defend myself by pointing out that I am in some decent ornithological company. The incomparable William Leon Dawson had this to say after his own observations of the Blue Grouse (known as the "sooty grouse" when he wrote of Washington's birds in 1909): "His courting antics, grotesque enough in themselves, are conducted with a gravity which makes them even more absurd." Dawson continues, "The cock works himself into such a transport that he becomes oblivious to danger, so that he may be narrowly observed, or even captured by a sudden rush." You see, it is not just the grouse's display, but the sad simplicity of his attitude that keeps us from elevating our entertainment to respect.

Tom and I found a displaying bird walking the mossy understory on one of our hikes in the Olympic Mountains. Just when I was lecturing Tom that we were not to be fooled by the insistent hooting that seemed to float from just off the trail, that we must adhere to the task at hand if we were to reach our alpine lake destination, Tom scanned the woods and—this is just like him—spotted the bird instantly, right off the trail. He readied his camera and sidled up to the grouse on his belly. The cock never missed a step or a hoot, just kept plodding in nearsighted circles, air sacs fluffed, nearly brushing Tom's nose with his proud, fanned tail.

I find myself shaking my head at the absurd bird, at the same time unable to take my eyes off it, or believe our good fortune in finding it. I secretly hope that the Blue Grouse hen, surely nearby and watching, shares some of my high-minded female thoughts about the antics of her would-be mate. But it seems that this is not the case. The more vibrant, loud, and outlandish the display in the grouse world, it appears, the more likely you are to win an excited, enamored hen.

I am not proud of my grouse ambivalence. I have all manner of reasons to love the bird better, in particular the ecological harmony that it achieves so effortlessly. And my worries over its vulnerability are sincere. The Blue Grouse is twined and wedded to Douglas fir forests—true layered forests, not the monoculture tree farms replacing them acre for acre. Its numbers in the Pacific Northwest are declining significantly.

Perhaps someday I will do better. Perhaps the particular absurdity of my grouse arrogance will finally be driven home. After all, how often will the Blue Grouse hoot snugly from its tree, secure in its affairs, while I, clearly the superior animal, walk in circles, scratching my head like the dimwitted hound in a Warner Brothers cartoon and muttering to myself, "Which way did he go? Which way did he go?"

The Secret Lives of Vaux's Swift

Open sky over woodlands, lakes, and rivers. This is the "habitat" description for the Vaux's Swift in a prominent book on the natural history of North American birds. The statement gave me pause. For one thing, I'd never seen "open sky" characterized as habitat. In most guidebooks, habitat is a tangible substrate, an account of the kind of place you would go to find a particular bird or animal. In simplest terms, it is the place an animal makes its life, the nexus of its ecological relationships with other organisms and the wider landscape. So fields of purple thistle are goldfinch habitat, and ancient forests are Northern Spotted Owl habitat. And though most birds fly, we do not call the "open sky" their habitat.

"Open sky" rings even stranger when used to describe habitat for the Vaux's Swift in its North American breeding range, mainly the Cascadian West. I associate this bird with ancient trees and coastal forests, summer lakes, and suburban skylines. Most of us hardly think of this region, the Pacific Northwest, as "Open Sky Country."

Yet I realize now that my concepts of both regional description and habitat possibilities have been needlessly limited. I was not thinking high enough. Near the edges of the water or the grasses, above the tops of the trees quivering always in their own breezes, up where we look to see the swallows flying, and then higher still: this is the true home of the Vaux's Swift.

This swift is a bird of secrets. Here in the West, where swifts are not terribly common, most people will never even see one. Among those who do find themselves in the presence of a swift, most will not know it. Of the small number who realize that they are watching swifts, many, like my parents, will call them "chimney swifts," even though the nearest real Chimney Swift is about 800 miles away. This is a reasonable mistake. While the Vaux's Swift is rather obscure, the Chimney Swift has a kind of fame; and since folks encounter the Vaux's in their chimney's flue, or hear of neighbors who have, why would they call it anything else?

Meanwhile, that eccentric and wonderful contingent who traipse the continent toting binoculars and field guides knows full well they are seeing a Vaux's Swift. They know the curve of its wing, the shape of its flight. From earth they can turn an ear skyward and mutter, "Swift, probably Vaux's," annoying innocent bystanders who look up, look some more, and see nothing. But even these rare and beautiful people, tending the swift as if in love, will never really see a swift in all its tiny detail. It flies too high.

On cloudy days, when the sky is pressed close to the earth, the swifts often come down to hunt insects over the water, dropping to only twenty feet above the surface, or even fifteen. These are the glory-days of "swifting." You can imagine that you might actually *see* your bird. But it's really just a tease. The details of the face, at this distance and speed of flight, are muddied; the gradations of color dissolve against the backlight. And the feet, your favorite part, are invisible. Where other birds fall to earth, mate on rooftops, perch on branches, affording us opportunity to set our spotting scopes on their feathered eyelids, the swift allows no such observation. When it is not soaring impossibly over our heads, Vaux's Swift drops with a spin into the hollowed dead trees that are its nest and roost sites. Lost to us, a bipolar mystery.

Though I have spent a laughably large number of hours ruining my neck to watch the Vaux's Swift in flight, though I once had the good fortune to observe a pair of

Vaux's Swifts mating on the wing, and though I want nothing more than to watch those tiny grasping feet at work, I have never held a living Vaux's Swift, or seen one through the one-way glass that surreptitious researchers set into the sides of snags for observation of Vaux's Swift nesting habits. Any morphological details I can provide come from those cloudy days of swift watching, from study of museum specimens, and from detailed descriptions in bird-banding manuals and comparison of these descriptions with that of the Chimney Swift, a bird whose odd little face I know all too well, having raised thirty-seven Chimney Swifts by hand when I lived on the East Coast.

Between 165 million years ago, when the first feathered dinosaur fell into the East German mud that would become the fossil record, and 65 million years ago, when the first known fossil swift did the same thing in France, evolutionary shifts changed bird-generic into swift-specific. Swift wings are exceptionally long and curved. Torsos are entirely streamlined, pointed at both ends, with no parts dangling off to create drag against the wind.

This is not typical. Most birds have bills and feet sticking out. Swift toes and legs lie close to the body in flight, tucked compactly beneath the feathers. The leg bones are foreshortened and weak, the feet tiny but remarkable: Four little toes point forward in an unusual arrangement known as pamprodactyly. With this limited apparatus, the swift is unable to perch in what we consider typical birdish fashion, where three toes point forward, one to the rear, curling neatly around a branch or an electrical wire. Rather, the Vaux's Swift hangs vertically from rough surfaces. To strengthen its grasp, a swift can turn an additional toe to the rear, making a kind of hand. Koalas do this, and certain lizards, but it is unusual in birds. While many birds, such as parrots and woodpeckers, have two toes pointing forward and two back, their feet are pretty much stuck that way. And whereas most birds have scaly legs, swift legs and feet are covered in a thin film of smooth skin.

Swifts are represented by some ninety-nine species in four genera, spanning the globe on their scimitar wings, found wherever aerial insects collide with open sky. Swifts are arguably the most aerially adapted of any vertebrate creature on earth. A Vaux's Swift spends its entire day high on the wing. Here it eats, collects nest material, mates, and dies. To escape airborne predators such as the Sharp-shinned Hawk, the swift simply outflies it, surpassing the hawk in heavenward assumption. Ornithologists suspect that swifts even accomplish some sort of rest or sleep in the air, though I am at a loss to understand how this is possible.

Like most swifts, the Vaux's is smallish, blackish, very strange, and a little bit ugly. Among the North American swifts, it is identified physically by its *lack* of distinguishing characteristics. Its plumage is dark gray and light gray, its eyes are dark gray, its legs and beak—yes, dark gray. The face is scrunched in, as if the bird flew fast and straight into a brick wall, a little avian Pekinese. Even as swifts go, the Vaux's is small, measuring only four and a bit inches from the tip of its tiny beak to the end of its stumpy tail. Remarkably vast in relation, its wingspan measures eleven inches or more. The tail is not observable in flight unless the bird banks or maneuvers, when it spreads into a lovely small fan.

Some authors describe the swift's feeding method as "hawking" for insects, but this word is best reserved for birds like the flycatchers, or some warblers, who set their sights on a specific insect and leap after it, catching prey in pincer bills designed for the purpose. In amazing contrast, the swift opens its tiny beak and stretches out wide elastic flaps on the sides of its mandibles, transmogrifying into a flying cavern that scoops up insects in its path.

Most swift activity is accomplished 50 to 300 feet overhead or higher, so swift watching requires a measure of patience and attention. If you already know that the Vaux's Swift is a swift, then you have a leg up on its identification. A popular problem is the confusion of the swift with one of the region's many swallow species. The birds resemble each other in shape and in habit, especially from our earthbound observation points, necks craned and aching, eyes squinting against a cloudy brightness.

The late Roger Tory Peterson even deposits the swifts next to the swallows in his famous identification guides, though the guide is otherwise arranged in taxonomic order. In fact, swifts are quite closely related to hummingbirds, and quite distantly related, in terms of evolutionary associations, to swallows. Peterson places the swifts and swallows side-by-side to encourage a ready comparison between these seemingly similar groups. "Swallow-like," says Peterson of the North American swifts, "but structurally distinct." While I appreciate Peterson's efforts to demystify birds and make their observation available to everyone, even folks with no ornithological background, I find this swift placement strategy to be both confusing and a little condescending. Surely any birdwatcher with a dose of native intelligence will eventually figure it out. (Peterson is in famous company: Linnaeus cemented this confusion into the early scientific literature when he identified the swift as *Hirundo*—swallow—in his emerging taxonomic system.) The swift is not even considered to be a passerine, a member of that large order of "perching birds" or what most of us think of as "song birds." The passerines contain all the familiar small birds—sparrows, warblers, finches, vireos, chickadees, jays, swallows. But not swifts.

To distinguish swift from swallow, look for wings that astonish by their length, that curve beyond any hint of a triangular shape. Find a little point where the tail ought to be. Better still, compare the swallow's fluid glide and sweet, measured wing beats. The swift flies like something altogether different—almost like a bat, erratic and tilting, but with its own "twinkling" style. I have found reference to the Vaux's "twinkling flight" as early as 1927, in Ralph Hoffman's wonderful *Birds of the Pacific States*, but it may be an even older description. Now nearly every guide uses this lovely, but distinctly nonornithological, word to describe the flight of Vaux's Swift.

Like many small swifts, the Vaux's gives the impression in flight that its wings are not moving in unison, that the flapping of each wing is not happening synchronously. Stroboscopic examination of the Chimney Swift has revealed that this is, as was suspected, an illusion. Ornithologists speculate that the bird's frequent banking and turning on the wind perpetuate the chimera of alternate flapping. Personally, I seem to see the asynchronicity when the swifts are neither banking or turning. I think it is just the strange, erratic nature of the wing beats that does not allow the human brain to smoothly fill the flapping gaps.

The Vaux's Swift nests in wooden hollows, but as much of the mating process as possible is accomplished in the open sky. Many birds deliver some kind of aerial or terrestrial display before the act of mating, but rarely with such abandon as Vaux's Swift. I wonder if the lack of color in the plumage and music in the voice isn't tempered by this extraordinary visual pageant.

Swift watching always requires some combination of effort, patience, good optics, and better fortune. Add "a minor miracle" to this list, and you have the formula for catching the swifts in the act of mating on the wing. Notwithstanding the fact that I lack patience, and am therefore utterly undeserving, I have seen a pair of Vaux's

Swifts mate, and will never entirely recover from the spectacle. First there is much chasing, dodging, and playfulness, coupled with a repetitive liquid chirp that is much different from the usual aerial prattle and is, I have read, reserved for this special occasion. Eventually, in an impossible display, the male wheels and turns and stretches his wings into a splendid V as the female circles, watching. Here, I am assigning reasonable gender roles, as there is no way of telling the sexes apart from my earthly perch. Finally, the female stops flirting about, and flies close to allow copulation. As they come together, the male flattens against the female's back. He wraps his tail around her, pressing his cloaca to the opening near the rear of her feathered belly. They have stopped flapping and free-fall, fast, seemingly fearless, nearing the ground before parting and rising again. In seconds they are nearly out of sight, high in the open sky.

The freshly-mated Vaux's Swifts collect nesting material by throwing themselves hard, in flight, against small twigs, knocking them off trees and carrying them back to their hollow. The twigs are painstakingly fashioned into a saucer-like mandala, larger twigs on top, spinning into tighter, smaller circles, spaces neatly filled in with pine and fir needles. The swift affixes these materials to the cavity's wall with a viscous saliva produced by a gland specially enlarged at nesting time for this purpose. Yes, this is the stuff that bird's-nest soup is made of, and it really does exist. In Asia the delicacy is created by boiling down the nests of a species not-so-subtly known as Edible-nest Swiftlet. One hopes this is a taste that will never be sought by the popular Western palate. I did lick the nest of a Chimney Swift once, and it tasted like salty sticks.

Four or five baby Vaux's Swifts will hatch from as many smooth, white, unmarked eggs. In days the hatchlings will be able to hang vertically from their four little toes, though they will still huddle naked in the nest, keeping one another warm. The adults will spend their days hunting insects on the wing, forming their captures into boluses—amazing insect meatballs, which they carry in their mouths to deliver to the swiftlets every twelve minutes, all day long, from just before the first light until complete darkness overtakes them. The pair will feed over 5,000 insects to their young in a single day; and before the nestlings are fledged, the adults will have made meatballs of over 157,985 insects.

Learning this, I began to worry for the nutritional well-being of the thirty-seven swifts I once raised. The East Coast is a very different place for swifts. There, the Chimney Swift is the common species, and there are many more of them. Unlike the Vaux's, Chimney Swifts readily descend into suburban chimneys, and countless city dwellers are made witness to the miracles of nature right there in the living room flue. Some accept the offering with more grace than others. The incessant chatter of young swifts has driven the less patient of our species to swat nests down with a broom handle. Overcome with guilt at the sight of the ugly, naked, completely helpless baby birds, these people deliver them, nest and all, to a nearby rehabilitation center. Surely *some* of the stories about the nests falling down the chimney because of excessive humidity are true. Whatever the circumstances, at peak Chimney Swift season one year I was saddled with thirty-seven baby swifts at our supposed *raptor* rehabilitation center. These I kept unceremoniously suspended from towels mounted on the walls of an indoor aviary—the terry texture was perfect for the vertically hanging young swifts, who are unable to perch in the upright fashion. I even took the nestlings home at night for evening and early morning feedings, having nailed bath towels to the bedroom walls. With their odd shape, scrunched-in face, half-closed eyes, curious vertical posture, and unearthly prattle, anyone would be alarmed at the prospect of sleeping in a room with thirty-seven swiftlets. My roommate Scott, a loon biologist, accepted the challenge with commendable poise, professing only a passing worry that they might scamper down and suck his blood in the night. He dubbed them, quite descriptively I am afraid, "scary vampire Martian birds from hell."

I made my own boluses for them out of Gerber beef for babies mixed with freeze-dried mosquito larvae (available at your local aquarium supply shop). Then I slowly perfected the skill of hand-feeding baby swifts. The swiftlets would crawl around, twittering and shifting positions, all day long. In order to keep track of which birds had been fed and which had not, I hung all the swifts from my own T-shirt until they covered my entire torso, then picked them up one at a time, tickled their little mandibles with my special meatball creation, and chattered—as best I could—like a swift. This combination of antics typically inspired the tiny Martian birds from hell to open their mouths so I could pop in the Gerber-mosquito treat. Each swift got three meatballs per hour. After its quota was gulped down, the baby would be trans-ferred back to the beach towel.

Once they were all fed, including any vagrant swiftlets that had skittered up into my hair and hung themselves by my thinning locks, an hour had passed, 111 meatballs had been swallowed, and it was time to start again. I enlisted special Swift Feeding Volunteers for the season, passing on the art of swift foster-parenthood to several willing and talented individuals. We did our best, and had a 98 percent fledging success rate, but there is one thing I am sure of. None of those swiftlets got 157,985 insects.

In spite of obvious physical similarities between eastern and western swifts, and notwithstanding the fact that I have just spent several paragraphs on a Chimney Swift digression, it is important to realize that the Vaux's Swift is not simply "the Chimney Swift of the West," as it is referred to in many guides. That gives short shrift to the bird's own evolutionary uniqueness, and to the particular "open sky" of this region—the one place, alone in North America, that the Vaux's Swift chooses as its migratory destination, journeying all the way from Mexico to mate, nest, and rear its obscure young.

Vaux's Swift is associated closely with the old-growth and later successional forests that distinguish the Pacific Northwest. It requires hollowed trees for nest sites and for the famous migratory roosts into which great flocks of hundreds, perhaps a thousand birds, swirl at autumn's dusk. Some hollows are the result of natural burns; some have been excavated as nesting cavities by large woodpeckers, such as the Pileated; some are the simple result of age and decay. Over and over the Vaux's Swift throws itself from high, thinning altitude to burnt-out, hollowed, decaying tree—and way down inside this tree. Though the snags are high, the swift will plunge down as far as it can, to within one or two feet of the bottom. This is no swaying treetop idyll, but an extreme nearness to the earth. A tree returning to the soil, housing on its way a spiral of migrating swifts, a saucer of oval eggs.

Some older guides proclaim swift nesting areas to be open, meadowish, watery places. These are clearly the easiest places to observe swifts entering a dead tree, and they certainly do nest in such areas. But more recent studies insist that swifts prefer and depend upon older forests, that these are the places of the most numerous, and most successful nests. Old-growth forests hold the past and future promise of trees in all stages of life, and the present store of dead and hollowed snags. As much as any other bird, the Vaux's Swift is vulnerable to the loss of ancient forests.

Unlike the Chimney Swift of eastern North America, the Vaux's Swift is not eager to nest in chimneys or other human-crafted structures, though it will do so occasionally. Even these artificial roosts are becoming scarce, as nice rough brick flues are replaced by smooth metal in modern construction, a material upon which the specially formed swift foot can find no purchase, and to which its nest-saliva will not stick.

Vaux's Swift numbers have noticeably declined in recent years, presumably because the tempo of logging in the Northwest has reduced the number of available roosts and nests. Thus the continent's smallest swift is currently a candidate for official listing as a sensitive, threatened, or endangered species. The long-term prognosis for Vaux's Swift is guarded. Fewer old-growth trees today mean fewer hollowed snags in the future.

The Vaux's Swift has carried open sky into the canon of Cascadian habitats. But it is an open sky that brushes, inevitably, the rooted soil of Northwest forests, and the consciousness of human watchers. In the secrets of its daily round, the swift calls heaven to earth, heaven to earth, heaven to earth. And the small black liaison glimpses us, sometimes, whether we are watching or not, from the corner of a dark gray eye.

Winter Wren:
Thoughts on Voice and Place

Listening to the voice of the Winter Wren rise from the forest floor, I am bewitched by a sincere belief that the song is very long. Minutes long. If someone asked how long I believe the song to be, and to speak my answer out loud, I might reconsider; surely imagination has lengthened the song in my mind. I suppose I would say that the wren sings in forty-second bouts. Or so.

The Winter Wren sings one of the most complex songs known to ornithological science. It is a waterfall of a song, bubbling upward from the forest understory, a series of phrases and trills piled one on top of the other. The song is loud and reaching, and the singer is as small and brown as a mouse.

I take my sister into the forest. I know where two different male wrens sing. Kelly is both a physics teacher and a volleyball coach, so she is very good with a stopwatch. She times the songs while we each make our own count of the wild, rapidly changing phrases.

"Fifteen phrases." Kelly announces her count after the timing of the first song.

"Thirteen," I say.

Kelly counts sixteen in the next song, I count twelve, then I get fourteen while Kelly gets twelve, then we both get the same. Fourteen.

It's not that we can't count. The wren is singing so quickly, we cannot think the numbers, cannot attach them to the phrases in our minds. *One, two, three*, this is much too slow, no matter how fast we whisper the numbers, or tick them off on our fingers and toes. We attach clumps of numbers to groups of wren phrases. It is like counting a flock of birds in flight.

We could record the song, slow it down, play it back, and count more accurately. But ours is a low-tech experiment, designed to satisfy simple curiosity. We just want a general idea.

Now we have a list of song-lengths. The average is eight and a half seconds. Kelly and I are both stunned. How can this be? The song runs on and on, it changes over and over, it lasts, it rings. Eight and a half seconds? Clearly the song suspends and expands time, meandering within its own created space. The watch says eight seconds, though the wren seemed to sing for a long minute. There is no explaining it, the mystery of Winter Wren song.

While listening for the wren, we turn our ears downward and our backs to the rest of the forest, a world of rustling ferns, unknown insects, the rasping of Steller's Jays, an invisible breeze that keeps every branch moving just a little, the quiet whispers of each and every tree. It seems even the mosses have a voice. Now that we are finished focusing on the wren, we take our hands away from our ears, and the other forest voices come fully around us.

It is impossible to know the birds well without learning their voices. It is said that experienced birders will identify somewhere between 75 and 90 percent of birds they encounter in the field by voice alone. In summer forests this is certainly true. Warblers that look brilliant yellow and black in our field guides disappear utterly into shades of olive in leafy, shadowy trees. Even if we hear a bird overhead, or locate a bird flitting through the branches, we may never get a full enough glimpse to discern its species. Turning to voice, we might glean the identity of an unseen singer.

Birds use a spectrum of vocalizations, the most obvious, lengthy, and individual of these being their songs. During the breeding season, songs are used to establish territory and pair bonds. Typically, bird songs are seasonal and they are sung by the males, though females of a few species do sing and some birds sing all year. Each species sings a unique song, with variations emerging within regional populations, and even among individual birds.

Learning songs, we listen for a variety of characteristics. Pitch is the highness or lowness of the song, the tonal rise and fall of the notes. Rhythm varies—some songs are fast-paced, some leisurely, and some speed up in the middle or at the end. The quality or overall character of the song is just a little more mysterious, but with practice certain voices begin to sound more sweet or harsh, liquid, whistled, or buzzy. With even more practice, songs can be judged to belong to birds of a certain group—a song may be warblerish, or thrushlike. Some birders are very good at describing songs with words, or thinking up mnemonic phrases that mimic the song to aid their own memory. Certain classics have been around for decades: "Quick, three beers!" for the Olive-sided Flycatcher, and "Oh, Canada Canada Canada!" for the White-throated Sparrow.

Bird calls are shorter communications used by both

sexes for a variety of purposes, including contact during flight or on the ground, maintenance of family groups, information about food sources, and warnings of intruders. These enigmatic little chips and whistles are far more difficult to attach to a specific bird than is an entire song since, arguably, they all sound very much alike. But some of them are highly individual, and learning calls is certainly worthwhile. I have walked with people who, on the basis of one tiny little call note, can identify nearly any bird.

I am not one of those people. I will never be as proficient as I would like to be at identifying birds by voice. Barely able to carry a tune myself, I lack an innate knack for listening delicately to birdsong, for "birding by ear," as it is called. Still, I study hard, developing whatever dim proficiency I am able to pry out of myself. I play tapes of bird songs while driving, I read call descriptions in books. These efforts, though I am compelled to carry them out, are next to futile. Field study, hours and years of field study, is really the only way to develop a reliable birding ear. For myself, watching a bird as it sings is the one thing that might cement a song in my mind. When I next hear the song, an image appears behind my eyes—the small bird-head tilted back, tiny mouth open wide, the voice, resonant and full, issuing forth.

Ornithologists typically study avian vocalizations bird by bird. Individual songs are recorded and represented graphically by the jagged, inky lines of a sonogram. The sonograms may be analyzed to reveal subtle differences between species, subspecies, various populations, individuals.

As a master field-recording engineer, Bernie Krause has been involved in the recording of individual birds and other creatures. In his memoir, *Into a Wild Sanctuary: A Life in Music and Natural Sound*, Krause tells the story of how he began to record ambient sound—the sound of whole systems—out of boredom. When the creatures he hoped to be recording refused to make themselves heard, Krause would just sit around. He turned on his recording equipment to see what would turn up, and to keep his mind occupied while waiting for the "real" creature sounds. What he learned could turn our understanding of animal voices on its head. When heard together, all the voices in a primary ecosystem ring in concert to tell a wide, wide story. Krause's life work inspired him to create a beautiful new word:

> *BIOPHONY—n. the combined sound that whole groups of living organisms produce in any given biome.*

In any primary ecological system—one not interrupted by habitat destruction, an increasingly difficult sort of place to find—there is a range of background noise. This is ambient sound, an orchestra of insect voices and botanical movement, occupying a unique band defined by Hertz frequency. Krause's research shows that in an apparent effort to claim an effective voice in the landscape, certain birds sing at a frequency above or below this band, at a "place" unoccupied by the ambient sound. Their songs occupy an actual *aural* niche, a vocal equivalent of the *ecological* niche so familiar to students of natural history. In every unaltered habitat he researched, Krause discovered that animals—not just birds, but many mammals and amphibians as well—have learned to vocalize in these vacant niches, unimpeded by the ever-present background voices of insects and plants. Birds speak with meaning in an "animal orchestra," as Krause calls it, a wild and vital biophony.

The implications of this research are, in many ways, still beyond our understanding. It implies, at least, another dimension of evolutionary complexity—vocalizations that have been shaped around a developing landscape for as long, presumably, as a species has existed. It points to deeper meaning in the relentless alteration of habitat that seems to be the human mission on modern earth. If bird voices have evolved to carry upon a specific frequency, changes in the landscape will alter the interaction between the ambient sound and the songs of birds. Species survival in the long term might be compromised as the function of song in gender relations and territorial management is impeded. Though a song sounds perfectly normal to us, in an altered aural landscape it may not be received in a way that makes sense to the bird or to the creatures that the bird's single life brushes. The birds, though singing, may not be fully heard.

In itself, *voice* is a layered word. It is not only an indication of the ability to make a sensible sound, but the continuation of that sound onto another plane. A voice has form and, further, it has weight. It has the propensity to interact with a world beyond its origin, and to have effect and purpose in that world. Krause's findings suggest a deep twining between song and place, between an animal's voice and the integrity of the landscape. In this light, the voice of a bird, a single bird that we can pick out in the forest, is not a disembodied element of its mating strategy, breeding biology, and territorial nature. It is not simply a clue to species identification. It is, rather, a true voice in the widest sense. It is an articulation of the species' place in the landscape, and that landscape's wending, in turn, about the bird.

The Winter Wren is a curious bird, curious like a cat. It rarely strays far from the ground, and so we lie in each other's sphere, zero to six feet from the earth. When I hear the *kip-kip-kip* call note of the wren, and search beneath the vine maples and into the ferns, I often find that the wren is already peering out at me or, more often, that it has scurried silent and vole-like across the trail, and watches me from a perch shoulder-high. It turns its head sideways, as if listening for something. It stays.

The Winter Wren's song is a sudden bursting forth, as though it was pent up so intensely that this tiniest bird could keep silent no longer. I love to watch a wren in the moment after his singing, surrounded by a fresh silence, a jubilant calm.

The understory of ancient forests is preferred habitat for the Winter Wren, though good, mature second growth with a vibrant understory is accepted. The song, with its mystery in time, begins and rises, and carries and ends. Beyond the singing, at the edge of the forest, the trees are falling by the acre, by the mile, every day. Even the so-called ecologically sensitive logging practices, those that do not create the chaotic scars of a clear-cut, will change the physical nature of a wild place, will interrupt the tightly evolved relationship between physical forest and landscape sound. We have no idea what this will mean.

It is possible that the aural niche is not of any significant import for birds. It is possible that ecological changes affecting vocalizations may be perceived by a species, and somehow accommodated over time. It is possible that our drastic alteration of the landscape will, over an unnaturally short period of only one or two thousand years, press a once-common bird, like the Winter Wren, into a hopeless rarity. We cannot know. But we can know this: that every bird song we hear, every call and utterance, speaks beyond the biological needs and instinct of the individual singer, joining the forest's own voice for integrity, peace, and continuation.

White Crowned Sparrow

Sparrows as Mothers

All birds look like sparrows to me.
There are big sparrows, small sparrows and gaily colored sparrows.
But they all look like sparrows. Last summer I realized this was a
know–nothing attitude, so I bought two bird books. They were
filled with every conceivable kind of sparrow.

—ANDY ROONEY

It is the summer after our wedding, Claire is not yet con-
ceived, and all of my friends are having kids. That's what

it seems like to me, anyway. In these warm middle months, every human and nonhuman animal I see has offspring in tow. I've been explaining the concept of the biological clock to my fresh new husband, Tom. "It's more than a myth, you know," I tell him, stereotypically drumming my fingers on the counter tiles. "I'm not in my twenties anymore! My chances for conception are diminishing exponentially as we speak."

Poor Tom. As it happens, my young husband *is* in his twenties (albeit barely), and is unsure about being robbed of his romantic visions of a carefree youth. He thinks about it all, talks with me rationally, ignores me, argues with me, and apprises me of the current price tag on those tiny little shoes. Finally, on a weekend getaway to our trailer on the Olympic Peninsula, he takes me by the shoulders, looks me in the eye, and says convincingly, "Okay, honey, I'm ready. Let's roll the dice," totally calling my bluff.

Do I see sudden sweet visions of Victorian prams and soft flannel receiving blankets? Absolutely not. *Acid rain, extinction of species, overpopulation, children with guns, persistent pesticides, alienation of youth, the worldwide spread of McDonald's.* A constant, endless litany of such images strings itself across my brain. Tom is still looking at me. *Who am I to think I could pull off motherhood? Too selfish, self-absorbed, orderly, too protective of my privacy. Too utterly unprepared.* I sigh and walk out the trailer door.

Slumping into a lawn chair at the Strait of Juan de Fuca's shore, I try to sort it all out. The sun is soft in the

late evening. Harlequin ducks swim in long family lines.
Farther out, scattered Rhinoceros Auklets dive, and dive
again. Close to my feet, a White-crowned Sparrow feeds
her freshly fledged offspring—the young bird chipping
like a ringy little bell. It flutters its wings, begging. The
female sparrow, small and brown, twists her head around
to look me squarely in the eye. She feeds her baby with
calm, with ease, then picks some of the cracker crumbs I
seem to have dropped for herself.

I don't know why people talk about sparrows as if they
are some kind of ultra-common bird riffraff. Write about
the obvious, says one well-known writing teacher—like
sparrows. She deposits sparrows in a list of other common
things, like bread and hands and your kitchen table. The
truth is, sparrows are far from common in the way we usually use the word. No one would confuse a hand or a
kitchen table for a foot or a living room chair. But to the
untrained observer, sparrows are mistaken constantly.
"Just a sparrow," people have proclaimed in my presence,
casually gesturing toward various species of finch, a warbler, a bushtit, a wren, or even a small sandpiper.

The word sparrow finds its origin in the Anglo-Saxon
spearwa, meaning "flutterer." And though sparrows might
flutter, they are not flittish. Sparrows are quite steady,
finely plumed, and delicately marked. In his excellent
book on the identification and natural history of North
American sparrows, James D. Rising instructs, "Sparrows
are generally small to medium-sized brown birds with

streaks. Some, however, are not brown." I love it. All sparrows are brown, except the ones that aren't. But this is the true language of sparrow observation—reserved and quiet, shades of chestnut, reflecting the particularly subtle elegance of these birds, and the habits of their best observers.

Many sparrows are retiring, timid, and nervous in the presence of large mammals, such as humans. As sparrows go, the White-crowned is quite tame and approachable, with a breeding distribution that blankets North America. For nesting purposes, they like small trees and prefer a nearby source of fresh water, which need not be large. With these simple requirements and their calm temperament, White-crowneds are one species of sparrow that is easily observed, readily reproducing at the fringes of dense urban neighborhoods, as long as there is a bit of shrubbery in which to sing and build a nest. Details of its breeding life are well documented.

In migratory populations, the male usually arrives on territory first, setting up his boundaries with a spirited, some would say overenthusiastic, burst of song. Many species of birds will do most of their singing in the morning, rest a bit during the day, begin again at dusk, dwindle at dark. The White-crowned keeps no such hours. He sings all day long, sometimes into the dark, sometimes in the very thin midnight hours when all other birds are huddled and sleeping, then again in the morning with undiminished fervor. The song is familiar to birders, and even those who pay little attention to bird-song cannot help but hear it in the summer, though they may not attach the sound to a mental image of the singer. I have watched all manner of humans wander in and out of the local shopping mall as a White-crowned Sparrow sings loud and unabashed from the corner of the parking lot, where there grows a stunted, ornamental pine. The song is lush. A buzzy trill, then about three whistled notes, with a little bit of gurgling between the trill and the notes. "See me, pretty pretty me," is one rendition of the song that birders learn early in their careers. There is much regional variation.

The female will arrive days, sometimes up to a couple of weeks, later. She will respond to the male's fine song with copulation solicitations, bending forward and flut-tering her wings. These will be flirtatious at first, and will increase in earnestness as the season progresses. It is she who selects the site for the nest within the territory estab-lished by the male. And though across the spectrum of avian species many males assist with such tasks, the female White-crowned Sparrow builds the nest and broods the eggs alone. The male guards, and sings, and watches without straying.

Once the young are hatched and eating, he will help feed them directly, bringing about half of the food that is consumed by the nestlings—mostly insects at first, with a more varied diet as the chicks grow. After the young birds leave the nest, the male will continue to share with his mate their care and feeding on the ground.

I admit that as I ponder the two sparrows before me, one adult, one fledgling, it is my own preoccupations that lead me to project "mother bird" onto the parent. As male and female White-crowned Sparrows look alike, this adult could be either. Knowing this, I continue unapologetically believing it to be the fledgling's mum.

The youngster flutters, the adult feeds. *If you knew what I knew,* I can't help but direct my thoughts toward the mother sparrow, *you would not be so sanguine.* Up to 39 percent of White-crowned Sparrow nestlings may be taken by predators, including garter snakes, gopher snakes, ground squirrels, Barn Owls, Sharp-shinned Hawks, crows, and jays. Most of these predators are also perfectly willing to eat sparrow eggs, and certain falcons and hawks enjoy eating sparrow adults as well. To avoid creating a ruckus that might alert predators to her nesting place, the female bird will, if she must leave, slide quietly and inconspicuously off the nest. Returning, she will stop flying when she nears the nest to stealthily walk the last few yards.

Surviving sparrow young will likely be plagued by ectoparasites—parasites that lie beneath the feathers— including various fleas, flies, and lice. Internal parasites might take the shape of nematodes, or blood protozoans. As the birds grow, they are, as a species, susceptible to canary pox, pulmonary mycosis, and a virus that causes disfiguring tumors of the foot. The young birds will not even get a chance to host such plagues if, as is altogether possible, they first succumb to inclement weather or exposure. If an egg manages to hatch, chances are about 70 percent that the freshly emerged nestling will die before the following spring.

Why do you do it? I wonder over the birds before me. The White-crowned Sparrow is usually quite spiffy, with a brilliant white patch, outlined in black, striping the center of its crown. Now, at the end of breeding season, this sparrow's feathers are almost at the end of their service. Even the white stripe looks a bit dingy.

I can make no special claim to Sparrow Enlightenment. Like most of us, I have dismissed countless birds as "just a sparrow." So it's a White-crowned Sparrow? I've seen a million.

But I'm sitting here in a confused mental state with hair that hasn't been washed for three days, freckled from the sun, dust between my toes, and tears in the hem of my overalls. I am disheveled and ordinary. A sparrow bravely feeds her chick for me to see. What do I want, a Bird of Paradise? Who am I to demand something spectacular and gaudy and seldom-seen to be named "beautiful"? Here is a smooth, brown sparrow, rare in its one life.

As I consider, obsess over, and fear pregnancy and motherhood, I observe this White-crowned Sparrow feeding her young so *perfectly*. Beyond any question, and with everyday fearlessness. Sitting up straighter, I pronounce this bird to be as brave as an eagle, as beautiful as a Resplendent Quetzal. Tom would immediately call this what it is—a hapless and unfortunate lapse into sentiment and romanticism. I shake my head and laugh it off. "Come on, Lyanda, it's a *sparrow*." But looking back at the birds, it's still true. This baby sparrow has a gorgeous, courageous mother. She challenges me, a lump of human with a hindering mind.

After returning from the Peninsula, Tom and I began shopping for our first house together. Like all good sparrows, we decided to find and feather some kind of nest before laying our first smooth, speckled egg.

One-Eyed Dunlin

There are birds here.
I hold in my heart an absolute sorrow for birds,
a sorrow so deep that at the first light of day when I shiver like reeds
clattering in a fall wind I do not know whether it is from the cold or
from this sorrow, whether I am even capable of feeling
such kindness. I believe yes, I am.

—BARRY LOPEZ

I can see the Dunlin's feet—crossing slowly as it feeds.
There are a hundred small brown shorebirds on the boat

ramp, mostly Dunlins, but this one draws my eye. The feet lag slightly, the steps are a fraction more tentative than the other birds. I am struck by the slow, crossing feet even before I notice that half the Dunlin's face is missing. Balancing coffee and Pop-Tart on a nearby log, I focus the spotting scope on this improbable bird. First, I see, an eye is gone. But it is much worse than that—an eye, a cheek, part of the skull, all have been torn away. The Dunlin continues to forage, touching its bill to the chipped cement of the boat ramp at low tide—touch, touch, touch.

Dunlins are squat little birds with longish, drooping bills. On Washington's Pacific Coast, they gather in enormous flocks during migration, turning in waves above the water's surface. Feathered white bellies and brown backs turn and turn and turn with mesmerizing precision. The flocking behavior is, in part, a defense against aerial predators. Merlins and Peregrine Falcons are among the shorebirds' most pressing worries. Huge flocks are confusing to the falcons, making it difficult for them to focus on a single bird and take decisive action. A falcon's missed attempt is the likely cause of this bird's injury.

The one-eyed Dunlin looks and behaves just like the other Dunlins, except for the almost imperceptible slowness and, of course, the missing face. I wonder, is she aware of the injury, does she understand anything of her predicament's scope? A shorebird must be flawless—must join its flock with a perfection of speed and motion, must maintain a constant alertness, a readiness to leave earth for sky in less than a moment. Even in the best of shore-bird circumstances, life is a wary, dangerous prospect.

I am momentarily pleased to see that the one-eyed Dunlin's wound has healed—it is not bloody, not even scabby, but has resolved itself into some sort of hairy-looking, neutral skin. She has lived long enough for this healing, I find myself absurdly hoping; perhaps this bird will continue life on the outskirts of her flock.

Dunlins gather along this spit on the Olympic Peninsula each autumn—the last leg of a huge round-trip journey from Central America to their Arctic breeding grounds. The two-mile-long spit extends into the Strait of Juan de Fuca, shored up years ago by the Army Corps to prevent erosion. A road now extends the length of it, winding past the timber mill to a Coast Guard station and a small marina, where I park my travel trailer year-round. I escape Seattle to visit when I can. The protected water on the east side of the spit is a haven for waterfowl, seabirds, and shorebirds.

An invisible dog barks from somewhere down the beach. The shorebirds lift, take a few wild zigzags in the air, briefly assess the situation. Safe. They alight back on the boat launch. The one-eyed Dunlin does not lift, but keeps foraging—touch, touch, touch, beak to earth, picking unknown, unseen morsels, clacking bill quietly with small successes. Unable to fully join her flock, she is reduced to the basics, and ignores the rest out of simple necessity. She is round with a spare dignity, with animal grace.

My mind can't seem to help hatching a dozen cocka-mamie schemes to "save" the one-eyed shorebird. *I'll catch this Dunlin up and take her home, where she will live comfortably in my bathroom, remodeled into a little Dunlin refuge. Smooth stones strewn about and wetted regularly with salt water. Tasty invertebrates hidden so she can search them out, eat them up, stay busy. Maybe I will buy one of those compact discs that plays oceanic sounds. My cat will adjust. It won't be per-fect, but at least she won't wander around slowly starving to death. . . .*

These are unecological thoughts, and I immediately forgive myself for having them. I would never actually diminish a wild creature in this way. Still, it takes my widest possible vision to understand the presence of this bird as somehow perfect, accountable, necessary, ordi-nary, ordained by the breadth of wildness.

Where does such compassion come from, rising like rain—natural, unbidden, unlearned? Not from biology class, where I toiled with other young minds beneath a sign that read, "Thou shalt not anthropomorphize." The words were lettered in pseudo-ancient calligraphic script to give them the ring of biblical authority. Don't get sucked into the mire of animal consciousness lest it cloud your higher scientific intent! I waded through wildlife biology classes, where I learned to regard individual ani-mals as data points, and measure them in terms of their statistical significance. In ecology and conservation biol-ogy, individuals are subsumed by species, with species-in-ecosystems becoming the appropriate dimension for research and conservation. It's not all that with-it to worry over individual animals these days.

Yet it is on the level of individual being that we come into honest, direct contact with other creatures. As individual animals we all tend roughshod to the details of daily life—we find food, brush insects from our limbs, protect our young, avoid predators, stay reasonably clean, dip our lips to the water pool. We walk, and we look into each other's eyes. Encountering other individual animals, it is appropriate to feel compassion for the harsh terms of our shared existence—to witness suffering, passing, and to claim loss in our hearts. We can realistically— even scientifically—apprehend the ecological whole where death and loss are not equated. We can feel compassion for individual creatures rising deeply within and beyond ourselves. *We can do both at the same time.* It is on this individual level that I wonder over the one-eyed Dunlin. One animal to another.

I wonder—*Does she know? How much does she know? Did I imagine the quick flash in her eye—as the other shorebirds lifted, did she really steel herself against the intimation of what her fate will be? Did she, as it seemed to me, renew her effort to continue what she could? Foraging calmly, the tip of her beak stitching along the stones? Am I wrong to think her courageous? I swear I saw the flash. I don't know.*

That night Tom and I take a walk down the spit, facing a wild sunset over the Strait of Juan de Fuca. We spot an immature Peregrine Falcon on the cellular phone tower, where they are known to roost. The young bird ruffles its scapulars, twists its head to regard the crows that are pelting it with their black bodies. It's a small falcon, probably a male. Confused face, quizzical eyes, worrying over the crows—this bird has not yet mastered the keen, distant gaze of the dark-eyed adult falcon. Through binoculars Tom observes the Peregrine, the very first he has ever seen. "Impressive," he acknowledges. But actually this bird is quite scruffy—the tips of its primary feathers are ragged, its plumage pale, faded.

In the morning boisterous crows alert me to the Peregrine overhead, flying for open water, talons clenched around a smaller bird body. The dead bird's legs trail, as if boneless, into the wind. I lose the falcon and lower my binoculars. My thoughts border on a hope that the Peregrine had swiftly culled the one-eyed Dunlin, sparing her weeks of increasing starvation and confusion. But that night I see the bird on the side of the road, alone now, drinking from a mud puddle. Oil from the many parked cars has invaded the ground here, and rises in the puddle—rainbow colors around the Dunlin's thin reflection. She peers into the water with one good eye. Holy, simple, shining bird. I speak to her out loud. *"I have seen you."*

Puffin

Young Love:
A Back-to-School Story

Joshua Rainstar spits when he speaks. Even so, I have to admit that I find him inspiring.

At the Seattle Audubon Society, I helped start up a conservation group for high school students called BirdWatch. The goal was not to create a bunch of brilliant young birders so much as it was to use birds as a jumping-off point for exploring issues in conservation biology, environmental activism, Northwest natural history, and enjoying the natural world. It was great. While recruiting students to BirdWatch I heard about a young birder with a beautiful name—Joshua Rainstar.

Others in the office who had met him and been on field trips with him said he was a decent birder, a good kid, a little lost, a bit stuck-up about his birding skills, a touch annoying. He sounded perfect. Most of the students coming to the program were new to birding—it would be nice to have someone with some background who might take a leadership role. I call Joshua, who lets me know promptly that he prefers to communicate via e-mail since he is "hard to reach" in the daytime and answers his communiques in the deep night. So, using the latest developments in computer technology, we set up a meeting at my office.

Joshua is a cutie. Tall, tousled brown hair, sort of a Patagonia dresser. At the risk of sounding shallow, I will say that this was encouraging to me. When creating a youthful image for naturalist pursuits, you want to promote an atmosphere in which it is perfectly wonderful to possess a traditionally nerdish appearance, but also convey the sense that this is not *required*.

Once he shows up at the Audubon office, Joshua eyes me suspiciously. There is only one thing in his book that inspires any kind of admiration, and that is birding skill. He throws some birdish questions my way, quizzing me not-so-surreptitiously. Playing the game, I throw around a little birder's lingo, drop the names of a few up-to-the-minute rarities sighted in our region. It works—I am, if not impressive, at least "in," and we fall into easy conversation.

Joshua's eyes dart around the room, taking in my office adornments—nests, bird skulls, disembodied owl wings, fossils, posters promoting shade-grown coffee for songbird well-being. Then he gives it to me straight. "I don't care about conservation or any of that. I'm a twitcher. I want a long life list. I'm just telling you. That's all cool," he waves his hand around the office, taking in the whole of anything having to do with natural history and conservation, "I still want to be in your group." Oh thanks, Joshua. "I want to do anything about birds—anything."

Joshua has braces, and he speaks quickly and mumbly. When he gets going about birds, he talks extremely fast, forgets to swallow, the braces get in the way, and he sort of spits.

Between my admonitions to work in an occasional quick swallow, Joshua unfolds his plan. He has an after-school job and is saving his pennies. In preparation for graduation he wants to buy a $900 car and a $3,000 laptop. The car will get him around the country, and the computer will allow him to check the rare bird alerts from state to state, help him plan his route. Minutes after the bell for his last class rings, Joshua will take to the road. Graduation ceremonies? Diploma? Joshua cannot be bothered by such trivialities. By the time his be-gowned classmates are processing to "Pomp and Circumstance,"

Joshua will already be on day three of his Big Year.

A birder's Big Year is a 365-day car cruise around the continent, a year spent building as long a list of avian species seen or heard as humanly possible. With his background and the newly available information highway (birdwatchers keep in constant touch about recent sightings on various rare bird alert sites), Joshua feels that he has a pretty good chance of setting a new record, at least for his age bracket. He's probably right, and I think this is as good a way as any to spend a year before going to college. Maybe we should all have done something like this, following our own dream and collecting our thoughts before being cycled into the higher education system. But this is where my worries over Joshua set in. I discover that college is not in Joshua's plan for his future, not after the Big Year, not ever.

"I don't need that. I'm going to be a bird guide. Arizona, the tropics, somewhere, show the rich bird-nerd tourists where the birds are. There's a growing market for this, you know. I can do it. I'm perfect for it."

In part, he is right. A glossy stack of brochures advertising international bird trips weighs down my lowest file drawer. It's a burgeoning, lucrative business. I pull them out. "Look, Joshua. It is a growing market, but it's also growingly saturated." I flip to the back of several catalogues, where the credentials of the guides are spelled out. "Look at the backgrounds on these guys" (yes, they are *all*, in the twenty brochures on my desk, *guys*).

"They're all strong naturalists, not just identification hotshots, and they don't just have BAs, they have PhDs. Every single one of them. You might be the very best birder, but you will go nowhere without academic credentials and the maturity that education brings. Take your year, Joshua, and think this through on those long lonesome drives in search of badland sparrows."

I pontificate further on the virtues of being a holistic naturalist, not merely a birder, about how each bird is a unique biological being, each species represents a whole string of evolutionary adaptations and relationships, not just a twitch on a life list, and how . . . Joshua makes his eyes glaze over, and we both laugh.

If I questioned Joshua's claim that he was committed with some passion to efficiently identifying and "twitching" avian species, and little else, my doubts were quickly put to rest. On one of our first BirdWatch field trips, the group piled onto a chartered boat to explore coastal waters and, from a cautious distance, survey the perimeter of a protected island populated by hundreds of seabirds.

"I'm psyched for this," Joshua told me, wrapped in layers of polar fleece, including an orange facial mask that revealed only his eyes and a small portion of his mouth. He was the only student who looked like he wouldn't freeze on the chilly spring waters. "I need puffin."

"Not for your life list?" I queried.

"Oh no." Joshua was offended by the very suggestion

that he'd never seen a Tufted Puffin, a wonderful little black seabird with a large and brilliant orange bill (the very color of Joshua's mask) and, over its eyes, plumy yellow fronds. It was one of the birds we were likely to see on our outing. "Of course I've seen *millions* of puffins. I need it for my state year list."

Of course. This refers to Joshua's list of all the birds he has seen in this state for the current year.

"Do you *need* any of the other birds we might see today?" I guess I was glad Joshua considered the trip useful, at least, and we would see lots of very good birds.

"Nope. Just the puffin," mumbled the young man behind the mask.

Joshua quickly shattered any fantasy I foolishly cherished that he might spend the day standing near the bow, gesturing toward the waters, graciously helping his less experienced colleagues learn the birds in the boat's path. Instead, the would-be bird guide plopped himself into a deck chair, wound one more layer of fleece around his neck, and studied a field guide to the birds of Europe, planning a trip that he hoped might get him out of school the following semester. We passed some beautiful seabirds, most of which you need a boat to see well: Pigeon Guillemots, Common Murres, Rhinoceros Auklets, and Marbled Murrelets. The rest of the kids were pointing, and peering through binoculars, and looking things up in their books. Single-mindedly absorbed by German sparrows, Joshua scarcely glanced up. When he heard talk of puffins, he leapt to his feet, held his very expensive binoculars up to the mask-holes for his eyes, and said, "Cool!"

For the moment, I have to think that this lad is a bit muddled. Still, at the end of a year of meetings and trips with him, I feel, even more than worry, a little smile of inspiration. Here is a kid who knows what he wants right now. Joshua wants to find birds, and he wants to be one of the best people in the country at knowing where they are and telling them apart.

Joshua had to come by this passion honestly. At the turn of the nineteenth century, it was not only acceptable but popular for young boys to pursue an interest in natural history, particularly bird study. These days, there are so many other things raiding our children's minds, there are few positive role models for avid young birdwatchers. In Joshua's most difficult peer group, high school, there are no social rewards, no validation for his chosen activity. It's worse than chess club. So Joshua's birding pursuits must spring from the soul, from a kind of true love: not a love of money, or material things, or enhanced social standing, but just love—love of doing a thing. And there is much to learn from such a young love.

Joshua is still several years from twenty. I have every expectation that he will figure this all out, compose a thriving life for himself. But I do hope that nothing ever wrings this strange and wild inspiration from his heart, and I hope that his mind never *entirely* catches up. In such wildness lies the possibility of change, makes me remember something missed and missing, makes me want to change my own life. To be young and so passionate that you spit, and to be spitting about birds—surely it doesn't get any better than this.

Swainson's Thrush

Postcards from the Mayan Ruins

As I stare up into the western redcedar, a big wet drip falls
in my eye. I wipe it away with the back of my arm, not
smiling, and scan the branches for the culprit—a crow
perhaps? I am relieved to find that there is none. Full of
winter damp, the tree itself is dripping. When I lean close
to the cedar for several minutes, the rhythm of this falling
wetness that is not rain is revealed. The forest is humming.

In summer the fragrance in the Northwest forest rises thickly and throws sweet cedar scent right into your nostrils. But now the forest smells like autumn; the fragrance, still lovely, is pressed close to the earth.

Discovery Park lies squarely within the city limits of Seattle, but as always, it is easy to find solitude in the acres of grassy bluffs overlooking Puget Sound, and then the wooded slopes that wind to the water. I am alone. I don't hear a single bird. Usually in this quieter, winter season there are at least juncos chipping and irrepressible House Finches singing their year-round ramble. But today, nothing. I listen and listen, but as my anxious ear reaches into the forest I begin to realize that I am not only listening. I am also waiting. The migrant birds have been gone only a couple of months, but already I am waiting for the return of spring and the song of the Swainson's Thrush.

Swainson's Thrush is one of the genus *Catharus*, from the Greek *catharos*. Pure. "Just how this applies to the genus is obscure," bird name dictionarist Ernest Choate notes dryly, though it doesn't seem so to me. The group, colloquially called the "brown thrushes," is a study in subtlety. There is little conspicuous about the Swainson's Thrush. Its body is a smaller, more slender rendering of our most familiar thrush—the robin. Its back is olive-brown with a hint of russet-red, the very color of the decaying redcedar earth upon which it stands. Its breast is buff, and spotted lightly with the olive from its back. Pink legs walk the moist forest understory as the thrush turns over leaves with its bill, revealing meals of insects and worms.

According to certain guidebooks, the buffy circles of feathers surrounding the eyes of the Swainson's Thrush, besides being an aid to identification, give the bird a wide-eyed, "startled" look. But perhaps she would seem so, eye ring or no. The young Charles Darwin, finally reaching the tropics while voyaging as ship's naturalist on the HMS *Beagle*, writes in his journal: *It is wearisome to be in a fresh rapture at every turn of the road; but you must be that or nothing.* I will not put it past the thrush, taking leave of the tropics, traveling by wing an unbearable distance, falling again in this different moist place full of new ferns and needled trees, I will not put it past her to be startled and wondering.

The Swainson's Thrush breeds in the low- to middle-elevation forests in the Pacific Northwest. It is not uncommon, but I am always thrilled to see a Swainson's Thrush. There is something about it that makes a watcher feel both joyful and calm. It is the loveliest of birds.

Besides its gently transcendent presence, the most astonishing thing about a Swainson's Thrush is the male's song. The Swainson's Thrush sings in a swirling upward spiral, sings the sound that would accompany Alice as she falls through the looking glass, if she were falling *up*, into Wonderland.

It is a song worth waiting for. But I am not certain that I am waiting correctly.

Back home I search my field notes for comments on the Swainson's. Every year it is the same. The first thrush seen or heard is duly noted, usually with some enthusiasm. Through the summer, there are further notes on birds encountered, their behavior, their breeding activity, and a fair amount of sentimental going-on about the bird's wonders and loveliness. There is typically a description of the song that I believe at the time to be startling and original but that, I see now, is much the same year after year. Later in the season, a walk through the proper sort of forest will reveal "no Swainson's" and, later still, "thrushes apparently gone."

This is a typical approach to the observation of migratory birds. We note the dates of their arrival, perhaps some details of their summer routine, particularly as it coincides with our own. Later in the season, we perceive that they have gone. But of course, the birds have not just *gone*. They have *gone somewhere*.

The thrushes arrive here in the spring to set up a breeding territory, to mate, nest, and raise young. In the late summer, they return home to the tropics. For most of the year they live in South America, east of the Andes, and in smaller numbers through Central America, into the south of Mexico, and in the West Indies. With this north-south migratory pattern, crisscrossing the Tropic of Cancer, the Swainson's is one of a group of hundreds of bird species called neotropical migrants that are claiming attention in conservation circles because of their particular vulnerability.

The perils of migration are well known. We've all

watched nature programs on our living room television sets that feature highly adapted birds losing stamina and falling into the ocean of eternity. This is normal—migration is arduous, and it culls the less fit. But new issues are facing the migrants that are beyond their adaptive capacity. Migrants that survive the journey are faced by complex, interconnected, and human-caused threats in both their temperate breeding grounds and their tropical homes. These include forest destruction, atmospheric degradation, water pollution, wetlands loss, and human ignorance. In Central and South America in particular, human poverty drives all of these, and richer northern nations press maldevelopment in the form of pesticides, toxic fertilizers, further habitat destruction, and unfair trading practices as "solutions" that ultimately deny the good of humans, wild creatures, and ecological balance.

The ecological issues facing neotropical migrant birds have come to public attention only recently. In the 1980s the Smithsonian Institution convened a conference to focus academic attention on neotropical migrants. The admission that further study of this group was necessary was made only reluctantly (or not at all) by many of the contributors, and the papers were filled with the myths that, up to then, had pervaded the scientific community regarding these birds.

Scientific confusion over migrant birds is nothing new. The history of human zoological study is riddled with entrenched misunderstandings over the nature of avian migration. In 345 B.C.E., Aristotle was immersed in a strenuous series of zoological studies. It was clear to him that great populations of "natural kinds" regularly appeared and disappeared. For him, questions regarding this occurrence were housed within larger philosophical issues regarding an animal's genesis, its substance, and what makes a thing move at all. Witnessing the annual disappearance of redstarts from the Greek islands (a species that migrates between Greece and sub-Saharan Africa), and their seeming replacement by robins (actually a sort of blackbird, a bird that winters in Greece and breeds farther north), Aristotle postulated a theory of transmogrification. Redstarts *turned into* robins. It sounds like a wildly naive bit of speculation, but it is a theory that was based on solid scientific observation, and one that persisted in various forms for nearly 2,000 years. Only 250 years ago, a not uncommon view among Linnaeus and his contemporaries was that the annual disappearance of swallows could be explained by the notion that they were hibernating in the mud at the bottom of ponds. And though Linnaeus was busy creating a taxonomic schema that would influence all of modern biology, Aristotle's theories of transmutation had still not been entirely discounted.

Regarding neotropical migrant birds in modern times, we are just starting to dig ourselves out from beneath pervasive scientific myths based partly on entrenched preconceptions, partly on incorrect interpretations of accurate observations (very much like Aristotle), and partly—perhaps mostly—on historical barriers to study. These include politics, language, and ways of doing science that change radically across geographic borders. Birds traverse these borders lightly, humans less so.

The old science tells us: migrant birds are "our" birds, "visiting" the tropics; they simply "winter" in the tropics; in tropical communities they are marginalized, rummaging around, grabbing what food they can, since the resident birds claim a kind of ecological and dietary priority. Well-respected voices in the ornithological community even felt that habitat destruction in the tropics wouldn't affect "our" birds much, since they were already exempted from the optimal areas. This last view was particularly pervasive, and is still a strong element in much of the migrant literature. Migrant birds in the tropics are "fugitive" elements, *populations flottantes*—"floating populations"—excluded from the best food and habitat resources by the highly specialized residents.

Much more study is needed on the role of migrants in their tropical homes, but we are coming to understand that these birds are much more than fugitives. They return to the tropics in the autumn, a time when competition for food is at its highest, with descending migrants, their young, and thousands more first-year tropical birds all suddenly vying for food sources. Migrants must be adapted to stable niches, or, it is arguable, they could not survive. Migrant birds are ecologically twined with their tropical communities in much the same ways that resident birds are. Many defend their own feeding territories or make themselves entirely at home in mixed flocks of migrants and residents. Some have even co-evolved specific relationships with tropical plants. More than we ever imagined, migrant birds play a deeply integral role in tropical ecology.

The information about the Swainson's Thrush that I am seeking is not readily accessible. In all of the familiar books and monographs on the species, the activities of the thrush are considered in the confines of her North American breeding grounds, and much of it I have already learned by watching, as anyone might. But I have not yet seen a Swainson's Thrush in the tropics. The only trip that I have taken to Costa Rica was in June, switching places with the thrush, who had already migrated northward. My next journey south will be in the winter, but for now I glean what I can at the University of Washington's science library. Even here, much of what I am looking for is not easily available, at least not in the English-language literature. Simple things, like the makeup of the thrush's tropical diet, are difficult to come by. Still, I manage to learn a little, and feel richer for the effort.

In her tropical home, the Swainson's Thrush vocalizes differently, with a rounder pitch, a voice that will lift and carry through a lower, leafier forest. She often selects higher perches for resting or preening than she does in her northern, breeding forests. She modifies her diet, eating fewer insects, picking more seeds, fruit, and ripe sweet berries, letting their juice dribble and stain her chin. The color gives her a somewhat tropical look. She will follow on the outskirts of army ant swarms, rapidly consuming the invertebrates that such a raid stirs up. She perches in palm trees, a sight I can barely envision. She spends less time on soil, and none on mosses. She is comfortably at home in her astonishing, familiar surroundings. What seems to me a double life is, to the Swainson's Thrush, the seasonal continuum of one complete life.

I conjure and keep the images. Love of the temporarily absent requires certain rituals to keep it palpable. The face must be invoked, the locket worn, the letters written, the received letters reread, tied with ribbons, kept in a special corner of the drawer. Such tangibles, while obviously tinged by romantic abstraction, still manage to keep the beloved from lapsing into pure ether. When you meet again, you will both still be real.

The birds ask little of us, but if "owing" is appropriate between bird and human, then I believe we owe them remembrance in times of cyclical absence. For their side, so much more is given. Crossing with their wings our hard-wrought and meticulously drawn human borders, migrant birds smear these lines into meaninglessness, and with the improbable presence of their bodies, their round black eyes, they bear a relentless, intelligent witness to the felled forests that we have known, to the burning tropical forests we will never see. It is fitting for us in winter to meet their eyes in our mind's eye, to say their names when it is cold. *Swainson's Thrush, Hermit Thrush, Warbling Vireo, Yellow Warbler, Common Yellowthroat, Rufous Hummingbird, Western Tanager.* There are hundreds of species, millions of wings, pressing the hemispheres toward wholeness, even as wildness diminishes hour by hour. Our own small spheres might somehow widen to include, year-round, the birds that touch us in circles, the migrants that carry, each spring, postcards from the Mayan ruins in their feathers.

Crows

Crow Stories

Everyone has a crow story. When I teach bird classes, and it seems about time to talk about crows, I sit down and put up my feet. The rest of the class overtakes me with eager tales that begin, "Once I saw a crow . . ." It seems that everyone has a crow story. Here's mine.

One evening I came home and there on the couch I found my husband, Tom, with a freshly fledged crow sitting calmly in his lap. They were busy watching *Star Trek: The Next Generation;* since Captain Jean-Luc Picard was in the midst of an absorbing monologue, they hardly registered my arrival, but finally they both glanced my way, Tom looking a bit sheepish, the crow nibbling bits from a can of gourmet cat food. I thought of something Bernd Heinrich wrote, inspired by his raven studies, "Living with another creature, you naturally feel closer to it the more activities that can be shared, especially important activities like watching TV." I smiled indulgently.

"You can't keep him, you know that, right?"

"But he can't fly, I had to rescue him, he was flopping about the yard."

"Of course he can't fly, he's a baby. You two can finish watching your show, then that crow is going back to his tree."

It's a common misconception that something is wrong with the baby birds that tumble to earth each spring, unable as yet to fly. They look a lot like adults, with most of their feathers grown fresh and new. We think they ought to be able to fly. Looking a little closer, we might see downy fluffs here and there, especially above the eyes, and a fleshy gape at the base of the bill, sometimes brightly colored yellow or, as on crows, pink. These are fledglings, throwing themselves exuberantly from their nests, ready or not. Flapping their neophyte wings, some actually accomplish a sort of beginning flight, some flutter gently to earth, and others plunge quickly to the ground, not ready to fly at all for another week or so. They will fluff and twitter, and will continue to be carefully tended by their parents.

The proper thing to do when happening upon such a bird is to wish it well, and leave it completely alone. No one can take better care of it than its bird mom and dad. If the fledgling is in immediate danger from cats or raccoons, or marauding small children, then forget that ridiculous and unfortunate myth that one of your aunts told you—that a parent bird will "smell human" on its baby and abandon it. Pick that little bird up and put it in its nest if you know where it is, or on a nearby branch. Birds do not have the best olfactory sense, certainly not one developed enough to sniff out "human" on their chick. Even if they did, they wouldn't care in the least. Birds are devoted parents. I hate to think how many baby birds have met certain death under the auspices of this myth, hauled home to be "raised" by humans who think it will be good for their own children to oversee such a project. It is impossibly difficult to provide the delicate balance of climatic and nutritional needs required by a baby bird.

So after Jean-Luc wisely guided his crew through another harmonious intergalactic lesson, we took Tom's little crow out to the apple tree and placed him on a high branch, close to the trunk, where he huddled with wide eyes.

The bird's mama crow, cawing loudly overhead, hated Tom forever. Whenever he left the house, mama crow would dive-bomb his scalp continuously, following him up to ten blocks away before returning to guard her fledgling. She had watched both of us put the bird back, but clearly knew that Tom was to blame for the kidnapping. It became obvious that she recognized Tom even apart from association with our house. If he was walking home, she would spot him blocks away and rush to greet him with a series of shrieks and swoops. Tom wore a bicycle helmet outdoors until September, when the young crow, whom we called Barry (after Richard Dreyfuss's son in *Close Encounters*), was a grown adolescent. Finally, mama relaxed.

In Tom's defense, I'll say that Barry was a difficult case. While most stumbling fledglings are quite normal, Barry may have suffered some bruising on his first fall from the nest, or possibly had some other problem with the development of his leg muscles. While his crow colleagues were all mastering the art of flight and landing, Barry was still having terrible trouble. We had to carry him out of traffic several times, and for months continued to recognize him by his particularly bad landings.

My friend Maria was also assaulted during the fledgling season by a crow that nested in her yard; but unlike Tom, she couldn't figure out what triggered the onset of the attacks. One morning she was able to walk outside unmolested, and that afternoon, and every day for the following month, she was dive-bombed. Wracking her brain, Maria told me that the only change she could come up with was her new haircut. In the morning she had her old hairstyle, and in the afternoon she had bangs.

A friend of hers was also being crow-bombed.

"Um, does she have bangs?" I ventured.

"Yeah, she does."

Most birds are more aggressive during the spring sea-son, defending territories, nests, and young. The large and social birds in the corvid family—the jays, crows, mag-pies, and ravens—are particularly so, and never more than during that one week when their fledglings are flapping vulnerably about our yards. And while they appear menac-ing, especially to a culture that carries Hitchcockian crow thoughts in the back of its collective mind, the swoops at our heads are mainly symbolic. You might feel a windy whoosh in your hair as the crow passes, but instances of actual foot rakes across the scalp are, while not unheard of, quite rare.

Not all crow stories involve perceived attacks, of course. Once I saw a crow walking around a daisy flower, pulling its petals off, delicately, one by one. Once I saw a crow gently preening a House Finch, an extremely rare case of intraspecies grooming. Once, when a Great Blue Heron lighted for the first time ever atop my neighbor's spruce, I saw three young crows stepping from branch to branch in quiet circles around the larger bird, not cawing or menacing, just staring, looking curious and amazed. Once I saw a pair of crows near a garbage can in a McDonald's parking lot. They were dipping fries in honey mustard sauce before eating them.

Crow stories change over time. At the turn of the

century, the proprietors of sawmills near the Seattle waterfront kept pigs in the mill yards. Crows would ride on the backs of pigs down to the water's edge, and swiftly gobble up clams uprooted by the pigs' feet.

Though curious, this abundance of crow stories among so many busy people who otherwise have little awareness of the birds in their paths makes a kind of sense. Crows are obvious: large, loud, and vividly black. Crows are intelligent, so they really are doing comparatively interesting things, things we don't expect of birds, and so we take notice. Increasingly, crows are everywhere, and though urban dwellers might manage to wear some sort of psychological blinders that keep them from noticing most birds, there are simply too many crows to avoid these days. More than ever in the history of the earth, crows are with us.

The number of crows in cities is on the rise. In the early 1950s ornithologist Stanley Jewett noted that winter crow numbers in Seattle were growing dramatically, with flocks of twenty or thirty birds becoming commonplace. Today, that number seems ridiculously small. Across the city, autumn flocks rustle overhead and join great evening roosts composed of hundreds of birds.

At the University of Washington, wildlife biologists are trying to figure out how this population increase, evidenced in urban centers across the country, is working. Graduate student John Withey tells me that here in the greater Seattle area, crow numbers are growing exponentially, curiously mimicking the human growth rate. But when taken alone, reproduction and attrition rates of urban crows can't account for this increase. The crow population growth in the city exceeds the numbers expected by nesting surveys. Where are these crows coming from?

Cities possess many crow amenities—lots of edible garbage, warm roosts, green spaces. But for a crow ready to nest and raise young, the suburbs provide even better resources: wider territory, fresh and nutritious roadkills, cleaner air, fewer cars. It's possible that some crows are having babies in the suburbs, then these young crows, as adolescents, are moving into the city for easy pickings. Crows don't breed until they are about four years of age, and they might live it up in urban centers during the wildness of youth, then settle into the suburbs to breed. They might stay there, rearing young that will themselves leave for a stint of city life; or these breeders might return to the city for the winter. This is one of the questions the UW researchers are trying to resolve. But one thing is certain. Most birds cannot thrive on the periphery of pavement. Crows can. And the more of it we make, the more crows there will be.

One good thing about the presence of all these crows is the opportunity it affords us to spy on a stunning, canny bird. We are rarely denied the intellectual challenge, these days, of looking out the window and asking ourselves the unanswerable—*what on earth is that crow doing?*

Crows might get disgruntled and protective, but at least they are not shy. They are extremely watchable, and their behavioral qualities are among the most complex in the nonhuman world.

It is not difficult to catch waterbirds in their courtship displays during the proper season, but for most other birds, subtle and secretive, we have to sneak and crouch and drive to far places, and get cold waiting in the woods. Or we can just walk out the door in spring to see the male crow in the midst of his wooing. His posture is stooped, his tail spread, his feathers fluffed; he is bobbing up and down, head bowed, and he is gurgling. It is impossible that the female he unabashedly faces could pass him up. The mated pair will perch close to one another, talking in crow whispers and gently preening the backs of each other's necks, the space behind the eyes, the base of the bill. Crows make no secret of the bulky nests they build together of sticks and bark, often placing them right in the branches of the hawthorn trees that line city sidewalks. Crow nests are usually at least ten feet up, close to the trunk, and if we could peer inside them, we would see that they are lined with mud and soft things: grass, mosses, small feathers. In winter we find them easily, large dark balls left in the leafless trees.

Four or five or six blue-green eggs are incubated by the female, with the young emerging at sunrise in just under three weeks. And while the nestlings are tended and fed primarily by the parents, crows might, in an arrangement that is uncommon in the animal world, be assisted by "helpers." These are believed to be the pair's offspring that have remained on the territory from the previous year. They support the parents in guarding the nest, mobbing predators, and possibly feeding the chicks. Nests with helpers are known to fledge more young, and the practice is likely to make the helpers more successful when, in a couple of years, they are ready to breed themselves.

Crows eat almost anything. Good, freshly dead fleshy things are preferred—frogs, baby birds, earthworms, slugs, spiders, insects, and snails. Small garden snakes are eaten directly, while larger wiggly ones are dropped from a height to kill or stun them. This fresh-meat diet is supplemented by carrion, garbage, seeds and grain, eggs, berries, and fruit. And while individual birds demonstrate their own predilections in terms of type and color, in general crows are partial to red fruit, followed in descending preference by blue, yellow, and green.

One of the things that impresses us most about crows is that they appear to engage in play, a body of activity we typically link with the most intelligent and expressive of creatures. On windy days, crows take to the skies for no apparent reason beyond the delight in wild flight. Crows will carry sticks into the air, drop them, let them fall, then swoop down to catch them in their bills again. Crow games.

The impacts of all these crows on populations of smaller native birds are unclear. Crows do raid nests for eggs and young, but so do lots of other creatures—the rest of the corvids, raccoons, cats, rats, curious children. Besides crows and children, most of these animals are stealthy and nocturnal, so we rarely witness the damage they impart. Crows pillage nests loudly in the light of day, and may receive a disproportionate heap of the blame for nestling loss. One day at Green Lake, an urban Seattle park, I saw a crow fly off with a fluffy, tiny yellow duckling. Unrepentantly tearing at this adorable tasty morsel before fifty or more horrified jogger onlookers, this crow did little to dispel the perception of its kind as so many "sneaking, thieving, hated, black marauders," as William Leon Dawson put it. Still, it is increased urbanization that threatens avian populations, more crows being just one symptom of the syndrome that such drastic habitat change brings.

So more crows mean more human-crow interactions, more crow observations, more anecdotes and stories. But I'm starting to think that it's not quite this simple. These crow tales we tell represent the objective, daylight dimension of the human-crow relationship. There is something more. With crows on the brain, I've been asking my friends, "What do you think of crows?"

"Crows? Oh, crows are interesting. Once I saw a crow . . ."

"No," I interrupt, "Not what did you see one do, what do you think of them?"

"Oh. Oh, well . . ."

A few, like my husband, appreciate crows unabashedly for their canniness, their playfulness, the ruminating look in their eyes, their beauty. And the rest usually follow one of two paths. On the simpler path, crows are considered to be intelligent and interesting, but also loud and annoying. On the other path, somewhat more common and certainly more complex, crows are intelligent and interesting, but also a little disconcerting. Not a they-might-dive-bomb-your-head sort of disconcerting, but an understated, intangible, evocative sort of unease.

Sometimes a bizarre scenario is imagined. One woman told me that crow bills are too large and pointed. A crow could fly up, try to get a piece of her sandwich, and bloody her face.

"Do you worry about other birds eating your sandwich?"

"Oh no, why would any other bird eat my sandwich?"

My friend Abigail told me that she was visiting a local urban natural area, the Montlake Fill, and when she and her two-year-old boy, Henry, got out of the car, there was a large flock of crows splashing in a deep puddle. Henry, entirely untainted by crow lore, was nevertheless frightened, and started to cry. Abigail would have tried to comfort him, but truthfully, the crows made her a little wary as well, so they got back in the car and left.

"I didn't think we were in actual danger, but . . ." Abigail told me, trailing off.

"But you sort of thought that, it sounds like. What did you think the crows might do?"

"I don't know. They might . . . , I don't know."

My wonderful friend Lori is the only person I spoke with who seemed both aware of the psychological crow dichotomy, and comfortable with it.

"I just love crows," she beamed. "They are so gorgeous and smart, and they scare me."

Lori couldn't guess the source of her fear. Perhaps there was something in a movie, but she thought Hitchcock's *The Birds* was silly, not frightening, and she could think of no other bird film, or literary reference, that might have impressed her consciousness. And this is typical of the slender fear of crows that so many of us carry, a feeling that seems to linger from some past encounter, when in truth there has been no encounter.

These interviews have opened my eyes to the crow tracks that crisscross us every which way. Our towns, our science, our stories, our psyches. And this might all coalesce in an abstruse sort of balance, except for one thing—the rift between story and science. In scientific reporting there are a few things that are disallowed. Anthropomorphism is one of those things. Anecdote—reporting of the non-replicable, nonstatistical one-time happenings that are the crux of crow lore—is another. While many scientists might *indulge* anecdote, most of them do not feel able to include it in, say, an article for a peer-reviewed journal. "That's very interesting, and personally satisfying, I'm sure," one of my graduate professors told me in response to my little tale about a crow I'd seen mourning the death of its chick, "but it has no place here. You know that, of course." The crow of science becomes lifeless next to the crow of the city sidewalk.

It is possible that crows will move us toward a blurring of these boundaries, a meeting of story and science, as it becomes clear that their varied actions indicate certain patterns of consciousness, capacities for thought, and even basic emotions—forethought, fear, affection, and a kind of anger, all of which science might find ways to accommodate. After all, certain ornithological treatments of corvids are beginning to admit "play" as a valid behavioral category. This broadened purview will more likely gain acceptance if watchers refrain from careless attribution of more complex or abstract feelings that birds are less apt to indulge—sentiments such as shame, pride, or remorse.

This morning, there are sixteen crows in our backyard, many more than usual. "Maybe they heard you're writing about them," Tom remarks. We watch them crowd into the tiny birdbath, while our chickens, who do not favor crows, cluck and flap wildly. One of the crows leaves the group and walks slowly over to the chickens' fenced yard. She walks around their wire enclosure, stopping every couple of feet to take a long minute, gazing at the chickens in complete stillness. Strangely, she has a calming effect on the hens.

I believe that our crow stories, and many other one-time observations of nonhuman nature, have value and should not be discounted on either the personal or the scientific plane. Without diminishing the sure import of the scientific method, we can also know that there are voices in the natural world that may speak only once. We are in the extraordinary position of being available to listen.

Glaucous-winged Gull

Bird Vision

*The birds did have knowing, and sang what the grasses
and leaves did say of the gladness of living.*

—OPAL WHITELEY, 1920, AGE SEVEN

In his book *The Value of Life: Biological Diversity and Human Society,*
Stephen Kellert unfolds his idea that we must come to
understand human dependence on nature and grow into
meaningful relationship with the natural world if any
semblance of earthly ecological balance is to be regained.

"We must dispel the great fallacy of the modern age," Kellert writes, "that human society no longer requires varied and satisfying connections with the nonhuman world."

He argues that the dimensions of human health and meaning—physical, intellectual, and spiritual—twine directly with a diverse and vital earthly biota. It is the realization of this interconnection—an enlightened sort of pragmatism—that allows for meaningful conservation. Kellert spells out his directive: "People will need to rekindle their capacity for experiencing wonder, inspiration, and joy from contact with the natural world and its many creatures."

When I first picked up Kellert's book, I was pregnant with Claire, and considering my impending resignation from the Seattle Audubon Society. At least at Audubon I had a clear avenue for service, and I felt useful in light of these issues. But all of a sudden everything was changing. I was wondering how to raise a joyful, compassionate small person, and at the same time rethinking my own role in relationship to the diversity of life. How to balance knowledge, grace, action. How to maintain a sense of hope that is meaningful, and not merely naive, in such an ecologically complex time.

One night, Tom and I took a sunset walk along Puget Sound at Lincoln Park near our home, and stopped to sit quietly on an enormous drifted log. We watched the Caspian Terns fly overhead, immediately distinguishable from the gulls by the downward slant of their heads, always scanning the water, and the unique lift in their flight.

Whenever I see them, I am reminded of a Caspian Tern I saw at the end of a long walk down a miles-long natural bar of sand and rock extending into the Strait of Juan de Fuca on the northern Pacific Coast. It had suddenly turned rainy and cold, and the distance back looked daunting to me, walking alone and weighed down by a day-pack, binoculars, and heavy spotting scope. I frowned, and nibbled on my last soggy bit of rice cake, as a group of about twenty terns nearby moved closer to one another against the wind. They stood elegantly on their tiny, triangular feet, nothing like the big flappy feet of their close relatives, the larger gulls.

There were several young birds among them, fat, round, and white, with large black eyes and gray heads, looking rather cold as it started to rain in earnest. I watched one of the chicks near the edge of the flock huddle against its parent. Then, in one of the most simple and beautiful gestures I have ever seen, the adult tern lifted its wing at the shoulder and, keeping it partially folded, held it directly above the young bird, creating a perfect shelter. I got soaked watching, but the tern was tireless. It stretched its wing just once in ten minutes, then replaced it neatly over its young. The sleepy chick closed its eyes.

Back on our log, I asked Tom if he thought Kellert's notion was possible, that humans might come into such meaningful relationships with unknown and even unknowable wild creatures. He looked across the water, then slowly began to speak: "Well . . . " But I'll never know what he might have said, because his words were interrupted by the spectacle unfolding beside us.

There stood a father and son, the boy probably about seven, the father on the high end of twenty-something, dressed in matching white tank tops and sporting the same buzz cut. They were using slingshots to shoot rocks at the Glaucous-winged Gulls settled softly, close to shore, on the evening water. Tom and I looked at each other and burst out laughing. Not because it was funny at all, but because the juxtaposition of images, of ideas, was just too timely, too perfect.

Telling this story to friends, they always ask, "Did you say something?" I didn't, the main reason being that I suspect it isn't appropriate to upbraid parents in front of their children, unless the situation is truly dire (and since both were terrible shots, the birds didn't appear to be in imminent danger). But more than this, I wonder what I might have said. The obvious seems so ridiculous. "You there! Don't sling rocks at the birds!" If you can't think this up for yourself, some pregnant woman yelling it out isn't going to help you along.

Wondering over this demonstration of what must be, I am hoping, simple ignorance, I am reminded of another thread from *The Value of Life.* Throughout this book, Kellert reveals the results of his extensive studies of

American attitudes toward the natural world. One startling conclusion sticks in my mind: *half of all adults in North America do not know that invertebrate animals have no backbone.* This finding is based on years of data accumulated from a wide spectrum of the public, including farmers, educators, politicians, and members of environmental organizations. Half. I am deflated by this news. How are we to accomplish the kind of shift in consciousness that Kellert so beautifully argues for, when the most basic of biological knowledge lies abysmally beyond our grasp? Does the dad with the slingshot know that birds possess backbones, that the bones of a wing share the names of those in his own arm, *radius, ulna, humerus*?

I want to believe that my own precarious optimism in light of such questions is founded. I have reason to suppose that this is so. Over and over I have been shown that if given an opening in the natural world, a world within which wild, nonhuman beings are making lives on their own terms, people will reach for it. When I bring my spotting scope to the water to look at birds, I am approached by interesting people over and over again. Birders will want to know if I've seen anything "good." But most are not birders. They are simply drawn to my telescope and want to see what I see. I offer them a look.

There is a float of Western Grebes, sleeping. They are black-backed and white-fronted, with necks so long that they must fold them back to rest their heads upon their shoulders, tuck their long pointed bills behind their feathers for warmth. If you don't look for them, they can be lost in the shadows of moving water. "I didn't even know they were there," one woman tells me. I focus the scope on a different bird, another species of grebe, tiny, the Horned Grebe. It is stocky and very cute, diving abruptly for fish. "I have some old binoculars at home," a young man tells me, a man about the age of the dad with the slingshot. "I wonder if I could see these birds with those, if I brought them here?" "Sure," I tell him, "sure you could." I am surprised, again and again, at how the simple act of watching birds becomes a kind of grassroots ecological action, offering a glimpse into a wider field of vision.

There are many other sorts of organisms, or geological formations, or atmospheric conditions upon which we might focus our awareness, with the same sorts of bene-fits, both for our own intellectual development and toward a sounder footing in the natural world. I am sure that watchers of rodents and marine invertebrates and stars and beetles and fossils might report the same results. But from my own biased center, I cannot help but feel that birds are a particularly well-chosen pursuit.

In birds, our murky ecological intentions alight upon a tangible form. Birds are everywhere. They are endlessly various, giving ready access to a sense of evolutionary movement and adaptation. Birds happen to be lovely to look at, and the ready, lyrical symbolism of flight and birdsong is lost on only the thickest heads. Even in the most urban setting, the presence of pigeons, starlings, and House Sparrows allows us to learn biological secrets of the avian kind, as they point like a poem to what is missing. Birds fly above our upturned faces, softly feathered, vital, and wild, every single day.

As we walk back along the footpath at Lincoln Park on the night of the Gull Incident, the sun begins to set, and the sky is full of unspilled rain. The thick, translucent air is simultaneously dark and bright. Lifting from the water, the Glaucous-winged Gulls rise to turn in slow circles over our heads. The strange light catches the undersides of their wings, making them glow. *Moments of being*, Virginia Woolf calls these, moments that somehow count for more, and contain everything, illuminating the more customary moments that lie on either side. "Look up! Look up!" I call to Tom, then realize I have not actually spoken the words, just *thought* them loudly. But when I glance at Tom he *is* looking up. "See?" he says softly, "The light on their wings."

Acknowledgments

My mother, Irene Haupt, has taken care of my daughter every single Tuesday since she was two months old, and it was mainly on these days that this book was written. I thank her with my whole heart. I am grateful to the rest of my family, all of whom figure in these pages—Jerry Haupt, Kelly Haupt, and my parents-in-law Al and Ginny Furtwangler (both inspiring writers). So many people have influenced these chapters that the rest of this list will necessarily be incomplete, but I want to acknowledge: Dr. Dennis Paulson for generously sharing his expert knowledge of all things avian; Sasquatch editor Gary Luke, whose intelligent, unobtrusive suggestions improved the manuscript immensely; and my literary agent, Elizabeth Wales, for her enthusiasm and her wise professional guidance. Finally I offer unending love and gratitude to my husband, Tom Furtwangler, for his technical support, good cooking, and entirely wonderful partnership; and to Claire, for boundless inspiration.

Author Biography

Lyanda Lynn Haupt was the education director of Seattle Audubon Society from 1996 to 1998. She has taught ornithology and birdwatching extensively at Seattle Audubon, Portland State University, and North Seattle Community College. She has also worked in raptor rehabilitation at the Vermont Institute of Natural Science, in Peregrine Falcon re-introduction in Minnesota, and seabird research with the Fish and Wildlife Service in the remote tropical Pacific. Her writing has appeared in *Open Spaces, Wild Earth Journal, Conservation Biology Journal, Birdwatcher's Digest,* and *The Prairie Naturalist.* She lives in Seattle with her husband and young daughter.